The Michigan DUI Playbook 2.0

Defenses, Techniques & Strategies

By Jonathan A. Paul

Chapters

Removing a DUI from your record

SELECTIVE CLIENT PROCESS
"SELECT 100"

Each calendar year, I have upwards of 1500 potential contact me for legal help. I listen to every legal issue, and assess every case, providing the potential client with my insight and guidance. Unfortunately, I am unable to help every client that contacts me for several reasons, but the main one is simply limited resources.

Because my approach to DUI cases in Michigan is so comprehensive, and geared toward maximum value, I limit myself to around 100 total drunk driving cases each year. This ends up averaging out to 8-10 new DUI clients each month, which I call my "Select 100". Although there are many other DUI attorneys in Michigan, I personally believe my approach is geared toward achieving the highest rate of success both inside and outside the courtroom.

When I agree to take on a case, I am looking for several components. The most important aspect I am looking for is my ability to make a unique and impactful difference for the client. There are clients out there who have been struggling with alcohol, and making poor choices because of it; those clients need my program to both learn from the incident, and to make an impact on the outcome of their case with the prosecutor and the court.

Most DUI cases have plenty of "bad facts", and it is a challenge to turn those negatives into multiple positives, but I do it on every case. Every client I work with leaves the case in a better position to move forward in a positive direction.

My clients know that they took every shot, and pushed every button on the board, and at the end of the day they knew their options and chose the path that was right for them. It is nothing more satisfying than hearing from a client month and years later; the client is thriving in their career, at home, and in the community.

Along with looking for cases where I can make an impactful difference, I am looking for clients who are truly motivated to help their own case. I can be their field general in the courtroom, but if they don't handle their business outside of the courtroom, we're missing a key link in our arsenal to push the prosecutor and judge to the point where we've maximized our efforts, and created the optimal result.

When I agree to take on a case, the client is agreeing to follow my proactive program requirement by requirement, and they are comfortable with my Shock and awe approach, not being afraid to challenge the case via pretrial motions, and at trial. The client needs to be willing to climb up the mountain with me; failure to do so, and we are going to come up short on our goals to maximize the result.

(2) SELF-DISCOVERY & EVALUATION

Once I agree to take on a client's case, it is time to open the hood, and do a self-diagnosis of the client. Most clients have a good understanding of their driving history, and their criminal background.

Although I allow the client to provide me with these details, I still have my team run my client's driving record and do a criminal background check with the Michigan State Police. With DUI's, it is especially important to know about out-of-state prior convictions; usually a client will have some idea of potential convictions from other states, and we will follow-up directly with that state.

Along with background checks, I ask my new client to share a recent resume with me, school transcripts if applicable, awards, evaluations and to begin obtaining letters of recommendation. I also request any medical history that may have impacted the case, and we follow up on anything useful to a possible defense.

When a client is charged with a DUI, the judge, prosecutor and police only know a few things about that client. They have your name, your date of birth, driver's license information, and they believe you to be a dangerous drunk driver. You can be 75 years old, with a perfect driving record, who drives cross country every week with no prior mishaps, and unfortunately the parties in the case will only focus on the facts at hand.

Therefore, we do the self-discovery and evaluation. It is our goal to shift the sole focus of the case from the "DUI facts" to a more in-depth look at the client. We need to know what the other side knows, and prepare to either neutralize a negative, or turn it into a positive.

We must take the case from:

Joe the DUI guy who was speeding at double the legal limit

to

Joe, father of two, married for 20 years, works at Ford Motor Company, had 3 drinks at a wedding, but also was suffering from the flu, and any test result was likely impacted by the illness

(3) 5-STAR PROACTIVE PROGRAM

If I agree to take on a new client, we have discussed my proactive program, and the strict demands, which I place on that new client.

My 5-Star program is nothing to take lightly. It is not quite boot camp, but it is time consuming, demanding of one's time and attention, and takes the right mindset to flourish. I can promise one thing, if that client excels on the plan, not only will they knock the socks off the prosecutor, and judge, but they will feel like a million dollars. We cannot go back in time with our time machine and change what happened, but we can control the future, and learn from what happened.

I tell clients all the time that in the end, we might have the case dismissed, or we might win at trial, but it does not mean we can ignore the incident. Other than the rare case where my client is claiming they were not the driver, my clients are typically found behind the wheel or provided evidence they were driving. These clients were arrested by a "trained officer" due to probable cause for breaking the law for a drunk driving offense.

While there might be officer errors (likely) or chemical testing issues (likely), there is at least some evidence that my client could have possibly used better judgment. The prosecutor may not be able to get over the reasonable doubt hurdle, but it does not mean my client cannot learn from the situation at hand.

My goal for a new client is to help that client avoid a repeat situation where they find themselves arrested for a DUI. Just because we "got them off" this time, does not mean they have the tools, resources and mindset to avoid getting themselves back in the same bad situation. I require my new client to dedicate themselves to learning from the case at hand, and use the experience going forward to help themselves and others avoid drunk driving situations.

Because my exact method has extreme proprietary value, I do not share it with the public, but I will provide this nugget for anyone interested in my help. Every client I work with on a DUI charge is required to alcohol test every single day, twice per day.

It is demanding, but it is the only way to truthfully tell a prosecutor and judge that the client is sober, thriving and complying. It is a positive sneak preview into my client's future behavior and judgment to assist them in deciding if my client deserves the benefit of the doubt. Most of all it is a weeding out process for selecting clients.

If a client resists this requirement, a red flag goes up, and I usually move on quickly. I know that we are going to run into issues with the judge and prosecutor, and my client is not taking this moment in time as seriously as I am willing to take it for them.

(4) External discovery & information gathering

Working hand in hand with my client is only half the battle when it comes to learning everything about the case. While my client can usually provide a decent recap of what happened, we need to dig a lot deeper in order to fully understand all the possible defenses, techniques and strategies.

Each case has its own strengths and weaknesses, and in my opinion, there is a way to win every case both inside and outside the courtroom. We obtain all information with three different processes:

1) Formal discovery requests from the prosecutor and police
2) Freedom of Information Act (FOIA) requests from the police
3) Subpoena power to compel witness testimony and evidence

This process begins the minute a client retains my services with requests to preserve time sensitive evidence, and a comprehensive demand for all evidence in the case (some which the other side claims takes a while to send).

We gather everything from the officer's police report to the Michigan State Police gas chromatography case file, to obscure evidence like the arresting officer's personnel file, and Datamaster training test results from years ago. We ask for everything, and follow-up until we get it; if we do not get it, we request a jury instruction from the judge.

(5) ATTORNEY-CLIENT JAM SESSION

No, my clients and I do not get together to play music, but we do get together to have in-depth conversations about their life, their future and their case. This term comes from Silicon Valley where phenomenally successful people, usually in the technology sector gather for hours and hours to throw out strategies, ideas, and go back and forth on concepts and possibilities.

Many of the most successful technology and media companies have been conceived, or greatly influenced by these types of sessions, and I take a similar approach to my client's drunk driving cases.

I have every client read this book cover to cover, watch my videos, read my website, and become educated on the possibilities and challenges of their case. While my client typically does not have a law degree, or have experiences with DUI cases, I try to have very productive back and forth discussions on the direction of the case.

There is back and forth during the hiring process, but we typically cannot get into the most productive conversations until we have done both a full self-discovery and evaluation, started the 5-star proactive program, and obtained discovery and information from outside sources.

The first jam session brings everything together and sets the tone for the rest of the case. As the case progresses, my client and I stay in contact daily, as the client provides updates on their progress with the program. During this time, my team provides updates on how things are progressing in terms of creating legal options. If the case is set for trial, then it is time to really get to work.

(6) PRETRIAL MOTIONS

I've yet to come across a DUI case as both a prosecutor and defense attorney that did not have at least one area to challenge with a pretrial motion. Unfortunately, this opportunity is ignored on 99 percent of DUI cases in Michigan.

I do not believe in filing motions just to file motions, but I do believe in challenging legitimate issues, and holding the prosecutor's feet to the fire on their case. In my experience, preparing well-thought out, and effective motions will lead to one of two possibilities.

One, the prosecutor who is already overworked will want to avoid additional litigation and will make a great offer to my client in exchange for resolving the case without the motion and evidentiary hearing.

Two, the prosecutor knows that the Defense is going to challenge their evidence, and hold them accountable, which opens the door for future resolution, but the hearing goes on for now. At that hearing, the client has nothing to lose, but the evidence against them.

Sometimes what I will do is send over "preview motions" to the prosecutor ahead of time, along with updates on the client's progress on the proactive plan. The goal here is to push for the "best offer" with motions ready to file, and real proactive success by my client.

The prosecutor knows we're serious about filing the motions, as it only takes a push of a fax button to file them with the court, and we've provided them justification to make a great offer by being proactive, and already being 5 steps ahead of the typical person charged with a DUI offense. Depending upon the court, prosecutor, and the facts of the case, I will either send over a packet with the preview motions, or just file them and go from there.

Ultimately this technique puts us in control of the case; we can take a great offer from a prosecutor, which would not be available without going the extra mile, or make the prosecutor show their cards at a hearing, and have the judge decide if they can go forward with the presented evidence.

The motions we file vary, and could be directed at the traffic stop, the probable cause to arrest, statements made while in custody, attacks on chemical test results (both blood and alcohol), and on a number of other issues. The worst-case outcome is the evidence stands, but we have now flushed out the prosecutor's case, and locked their witnesses into testimony, which we can use to impeach at trial.

(7) SHOCK AND AWE METHOD

As discussed in the previous section, I send a packet to the prosecuting attorney in every case with additional information on my client, positive updates on my client's proactive success, and a preview of the motions to be filed, or a recap of the motions that were filed.

This is a much different approach than almost every other attorney in Michigan. As a former prosecutor, I saw every approach, and I have never seen what I do with my clients.

The typical scenario plays out this way: lawyer gets hired, lawyer files appearance with the court and prosecutor, lawyer has first communication with the prosecutor on the first court date, prosecutor makes default offer that every other attorney receives. A client can do this themselves without the assistance of a lawyer.

By previewing or filing various motions prior to the first court date, it sets the tone for the rest of the case. My client's always keep the door open for resolution if it matches their goals, but the prosecutor knows that the default offer will not likely get the deal done. When a prosecutor's workload is about to go up, they will fight it by making it go away.

This might mean making an exception to a policy and going the extra step in their offer, which would not be available without this Shock and awe. This term is a military doctrine based on the use of overwhelming power and spectacular displays of force to paralyze the enemy's perception of the battlefield and destroy its will to fight.

By making the prosecutor work before the case even begins, it gives my client the edge needed to maximize the result. Along with showing spectacular force and confidence, we help the prosecutor justify their generosity with our proactive efforts.

For example, if my client's case has some negative elements like an accident or a high BAC reading, yet we point out issues with the case, and get the prosecutor to "deal" beyond their typical offer, the prosecutor still needs to worry about the perception of the case.

A prosecutor cannot explain an exception by saying "well our case stinks", because that is a negative reflection on the cops, and their office for even charging it. What they can explain as part of their decision is 60 days of documented sobriety by the Defendant, 30 AA meetings, 50 hours of volunteer work given back to the community, alcohol education and ongoing counseling among other achievements.

If we demonstrate strength, confidence and the willingness to fight real legal issues, and provide the prosecutor with the escape hatch to get out of dodge and save face then we stand a great chance of succeeding.

(8) PREEMPTIVE STRIKE

Part of the Shock and awe approach is the willingness to contest the evidence via motion practice and hold hearings on the evidence. A motion is filed with the court, and the court can either rule on the action requested or agree to hold a hearing.

At this hearing, the burden will be on the prosecutor to produce both witness testimony and physical evidence in order to demonstrate that my client's constitutional rights were not violated, and that the issue is a matter better suited to be heard by the trier of fact on the question of guilt or innocence. If a judge suppresses evidence this means that it will no longer be admissible at trial, and depending upon the evidence, a prosecutor may be forced to dismiss the entire case.

Here are a few common issues, which I challenge on a regular basis:

- The validity of the traffic stop/police detention
- Suppression of statements made by my client
- Challenge the probable cause to arrest and all further evidence
- Challenge the admission of the PBT and field sobriety tests
- Challenge the admissibility of the Datamaster
- Challenge the admissibility - Gas Chromatography/Blood

(9) 5-STAR TRIAL METHOD

If after exhausting our efforts outside of the courtroom with the proactive program, and challenging the evidence via motion and evidentiary hearing, we are still not presented with an outcome, which my client find acceptable, then we go to trial. A trial can be with a judge or jury, and that is usually judge and fact specific to each case.

Ultimately the burden is 100 percent on the prosecutor to present evidence of the "elements" of the offense. For most misdemeanor DUI cases those elements are driving (as defined by the law) by the Defendant, and either impairment or intoxication, which can be done with a chemical test result.

My method essentially all comes down to the five levels of proof provided by Michigan law. In my experience as a prosecutor, and now as DUI defense attorney, most attorneys ignore or simply skim over one of the greatest assets of a defense lawyer. The power of reasonable doubt is ignored, and a jury can simply hear the evidence and pick a side without really applying the law.

Here is what happens in 99.9 percent of DUI cases in Michigan. Prosecutor presents witness testimony; test results and argues that the elements are clearly met. Defense lawyer repeats many of the same questions asked by the prosecutor, and fishes for "yes it's possible" answers from the prosecution witnesses. Maybe they throw in some questions to take the shine off the test result and get the prosecution witnesses to admit some positive facts.

Jury still has the cold hard facts of driving and usually a BAC reading over the legal limit; that seems a lot more powerful than a few chips taken off by a defense lawyer, and well I don't like drunk drivers, so I am going to vote guilty. This approach will get you convicted almost every time, because the defense lawyer is allowing a jury to apply the wrong standard, and they simply do not know any better.

It has not the jurors' fault, as they were not educated during the jury selection process, and both the judge and lawyers threw out the term reasonable doubt without giving any context or meaning.

I am not going to get into the specifics on how I build that doubt for a jury, because that's why a client hires me, but I will do a quick demonstration on how the five levels of proof work.

The typical case only uses the term reasonable doubt, and the phrase guilty or not guilty as if they are two equal results. The cards are also stacked against the defendant in terms of evidence despite some chips knocked off by the defense team. By default, the "guilty" column is going to appear to be a lot stronger than the "not guilty" one. That is how people get convicted.

You can take those same chips taken off the evidence (or chunks if I am the one defending you), and put them up in the correct context of levels of proof, and with the right jury, you can win every time no matter your facts.

In Michigan, there are five levels of proof: reasonable suspicion, probable cause, preponderance of the evidence, clear and convincing evidence and reasonable doubt.

An officer can pull you over or detain you if they have reasonable suspicion a crime was committed, and you were the one who committed it. Probable cause is the standard for arrest, which means "you probably did it" based on the evidence. Both are not enough to convict someone.

You then have the three trial proofs. Preponderance of the evidence is the classic 51 percent rule; put the good and the bad on a scale and if the guilty facts outweigh the not guilty than you pick guilty. Clear and convincing is the next level, which is as it sounds, you are clearly convinced of the person's guilt, so you vote guilty.

Reasonable doubt is the last one, but the perception does a 180 turn once a jury understands what is beneath it. I educate a jury from the beginning of the case on these levels, provide them multiple reasons to doubt the evidence during the trial, then walk them down the five levels of proof at the end of the case.

Essentially, I give the jury a long enough leash if they wish, to believe it is "reasonable" that my client is guilty, that the client is "probably" guilty, that is more likely than not that they are guilty, and even that they are clearly convinced that the client is guilty.

It's a mistake to allow a jury to think about the case as 0 or 100, yes or no, black or white; you need to empower a jury to view the facts and say "yeah this guy isn't innocent"; if you fight that then the only other option is guilty. Give the jury room to breathe, and hold their hand up the steps of proof; tell them it's ok to keep going, but before we get to the highest level, they will realize that they can't take the final step.

You can't be afraid to let a jury walk away clearly convinced that the client committed a crime, but they followed the rules, and applied the proper legal proof, and found at least one reason to doubt the client's guilt. My method builds up plenty of doubt and provides enough justification to stop at a level shy of beyond a reasonable doubt.

I compare this jury ignorance of the legal proofs to a situation many years ago when a social experiment was done with a famous violinist and Grammy-winner who posed as a street performer in the subway while unbeknownst to subway riders was playing a $3 million instrument. He performed the same music, which otherwise costs hundreds of dollars to buy a ticket to see his performance live-in world-famous venues.

A jury in most cases is just going to go with their instinct and react in the most familiar manner. They hear 100's of people playing instruments in the subway, this 101st performer sounds similar enough to group them into my typical reaction; ignore it.

In a DUI trial, well the evidence sounds like what I would expect in a DUI case, there is enough there, and well the defense lawyer is being paid to try to get their client to be innocent.

An educated evaluator of music will immediately hear the difference, as will an educated juror. When put in the correct context, a juror is going to apply the correct standard, and give my client the path for a successful outcome.

(10) A-PLUS CONTINGENCY PLAN

If after maximizing our leverage and playing our cards, the client decides to end their case with a deal, then we will be sentenced by the judge. Most sentences go like this:

Client and lawyer show up in court a bunch of times, something is eventually worked out or the client is convicted by a jury who didn't understand the levels of legal proof, and now the client will be assessed, evaluated and judged by probation who will supply a recommendation to the judge for the eventual sentence. Same client and lawyer get a copy of this a few minutes before sentencing and can agree or disagree. Lawyer says their client is a great person, has a job, kids blah blah blah.

That does not move the needle, and the client is paying thousands of dollars for a glorified babysitter. I take an entirely different approach. As I discussed above my client is on my proactive program from the day we begin working together.

The client can be DONE with their sentence before even going to sentencing. Yes, you heard that correctly. I get my clients credit for their entire sentence on a regular basis because I know exactly what judges are looking for, and we are doing it on our own time without the hammer of the court. If the judge does not give full credit, they will instead reduce what they were going to sentence the client to, and again, the credited portion is now not performed on the court's time.

Along with having all of this in place, it must be properly documented for the probation staff and the judge so that it can be reviewed in advance of sentencing.

If you were to be sentenced on a DUI case, under which scenario would you like to be in when your freedom is on the line, and the judge controls the next 24 months of your life on a misdemeanor or 60 months on a felony.

Scenario #1 - showed up in court a bunch of times, sat up late at night reading the internet and worrying, but didn't do anything but worry for the last 6 weeks about this moment in front of the judge, and now you feel the urge to ramble in a mix of apologies and promises to never be back in court.

Scenario #2 - showing the judge just how seriously you are taking this case, as you've passed 120 alcohol tests over 60 days, you've learned a great deal at over 40 AA meetings, you are currently working with a substance abuse counselor to learn more about yourself, and make wiser choices, and you've given 50 hours back to the community in volunteer work to show you're a positive member of society among other efforts - you don't feel the need to apologize to a judge who was likely sound asleep and unaffected that evening, and you know not to promise a single thing, because you would have said you'd never get a DUI before this one happened - humble and optimistic about the future, you walk into court with confidence.

(11) CHALLENGING THE STOP
NOT A MOTOR VEHICLE

A great defense to a DUI charge in Michigan is simply lack of motor vehicle. This is a rare defense, because a police officer is unlikely to pull over or stop a non-motor vehicle as defined under Michigan law, it's in the law books and jury instructions for a reason, and it is worth exploring. As technology continues to advance the definition of "motor vehicle" will continue to either shrink or expand. It will be interesting when self-driving cars become a reality, and how this portion of the law will be treated.

In Michigan, the elements, which the prosecutor needs to prove in a DUI case are the following.

1. operating a motor vehicle,
2. on a highway or other place open to the general public, or generally accessible to motor vehicles,
3. in the county of *[county]*, city of *[city]* (venue),
4. while under the influence of alcohol and/or with an unlawful bodily alcohol level of .08 grams or more.

We get our definition of "motor vehicle" from MCL 257.79, which states that a vehicle is "every device in, upon, or by which any person or property is or may be transported or drawn upon a highway, except devices exclusively moved by human power or used exclusively upon stationary rails or tracks and except, only for the purpose of titling and registration under this act, a mobile home."

The obvious "motor vehicle" is what you normally consider a vehicle/car, such as your Jeep, Ford, Chevy and hundreds of other companies and models. It has also been held by Michigan courts that a "motor vehicle" can also be a go-cart, a snowmobile, a motorized boat, a dune buggy or similar motorized device. Many people ask me if they can ride their bikes after drinking alcohol, and I tell them under current law, no this is not considered drunk driving. If you are exclusively powering the bike to move, then you are not breaking any law.

(12) CHALLENGING THE STOP: NOT A HIGHWAY OR OPEN TO THE PUBLIC

Along with the motor vehicle requirement to be found guilty, the prosecutor must also show that you were traveling on a road/highway, which was open to the public. If you were not doing so, there might be grounds to dismiss based upon an illegal stop/seizure, or you could be entitled to a not guilty verdict at trial based on lack of evidence of one of the elements.

The law defines open to the public under MCL 257.625(1) as any "other place open to the general public or generally accessible to motor vehicles, including an area designated for the parking of vehicles, within this state." So, if you are operating or were previously operating, and you are now in a parking lot then the law still applies to your case. The same holds true if you pull into your own driveway; you cannot escape the law by ending up in a non-public parking spot. Parking lots and pit stops have been deemed "generally accessible to motor vehicles" because vehicles are routinely permitted to enter for the purpose of driving and parking.

A viable defense may be available if an officer finds you in a restricted area or on private property such as your driveway, but he/she doesn't have evidence that you were otherwise operating on a public road, which is open to the public. The prosecutor may argue that if you are found sitting in your driveway with the engine on, well you were previously driving, or the engine is off, but the hood is still hot. While these are viable arguments by the prosecutor, the burden is on them to provide the proper proof of that operating on a highway open to the public.

It is important to do a full analysis on the area, and who can enter, and who cannot enter, along with the hours of operation, and restrictions placed on the area. The more restrictions, and less access, the better the possible defense. It is important to consider all posted signs, barriers or obstacles for entering. If you believe you were "seized" by an officer on private property, this could be a defense.

(13) CHALLENGING THE STOP: NO OBSERVATION OF DRIVING

Most clients are extremely honest people who would never think to lie to a police officer. I agree that people should be honest, but they also need to practice self-preservation when it comes to interacting with a police officer, and any law enforcement.

A major DUI defense in my practice is pushing forward with the theory of lack of operation. This simply means the prosecutor does not have any direct evidence that you were driving a car.

Unfortunately, this defense gets blown up on many of my cases where the client is asked "were you driving?" or they voluntarily admit to driving. This question is only asked by an officer when he has not personally pulled you over or has another eyewitness to your driving such as a 911 tipster or witness on the scene. You should not assist in your own prosecution, because you want to be honest and truthful; let the police and prosecutor earn their paycheck.

Even without these voluntary admissions of driving, the prosecutor can present indirect evidence of operation such as you own the car, insure the car, and you were found in or near the car when the police arrived. If you are the only person at the scene, well then who else drove the car? Maybe the car was in an accident, or the hood is still hot, which would indicate the car was just running. Usually the police officer is not that lucky to have all these factors to help their case.

These are all theories that the prosecutor needs to worry about, and as a former prosecutor, I've used these indirect theories on 100's of occasions, but it still comes down to the prosecutor meeting their burden.

If the prosecutor has no direct evidence of driving then it's a true defense to a DUI; there's no lying or misstating the truth either, because as the defense we don't need to prove you weren't driving or even comment on it. Here is a quick sample of how I would present this theory in a DUI case in Michigan with an effective cross-examination of the officer. You will see that this cross-examination is NOT confrontational, but rather simply seeks admissions of uncertainty or truth.

Me: Officer, when you arrived at the scene, you observed both my client and two females standing outside of the car, correct?

Officer: Yes

Me: You did not observe my client in the vehicle at any time, let alone driving correct?

Officer: Correct

Me: And, upon investigation you learned that this vehicle was registered and insured by someone other than my client corrects?

Officer: Correct

Me: At any time did my client indicate he was driving the car?

Officer: No, he did not say anything, I kept asking, but he kept telling me he wanted to speak to his lawyer.

Me: And when you received your radio run of an accident, there was no indication of who was driving correct?

Officer: Right

Me: So, officer, you come here today not certain that my client was driving the vehicle, which you came upon that night?

Officer: Well no, but I am pretty sure it was him, I could just tell

Me: Again officer, despite your hunch, you have no direct evidence he was driving, because it could have been any of the three people, or even someone who ran away from the scene, isn't that correct?

Officer: Yeah, I guess so

If you are charged with a DUI in Michigan, and the officer has no direct observation of your driving, then there is uncertainty, which provides reasonable doubt to a jury, which should lead to a not guilty verdict. Even if you are the only one at the scene, I have had many cases where the real driver ran away from the vehicle and left my client holding the bag. The lesson here is always to not say a word and ask for your attorney. Handing your license to the officer is all you must do upon questioning of that officer.

For a defense like this to work, the jury must be properly educated on the correct levels of legal proof. It's fine if a jury thinks it's reasonable you were the driver, probable that you were the driver, 51/49 that you were the driver, and can be clearly convinced you were the driver, but if we give them a reason to doubt it, then you're entitled to a not-guilty verdict by law.

(14) CHALLENGING THE STOP: NO REASONABLE SUSPICION - TRAFFIC VIOLATION

The most common start to a Michigan DUI offense is with a traffic stop conducted by a police officer for a violation of a traffic offense. In Michigan MCL 257.724(1) allows a police officer to stop a vehicle, detain a driver and issue a citation for any witnessed violation of the Michigan Vehicle Code or civil infraction.

Without a violation of the Vehicle Code, an officer is required to have an 'individualized, articulable suspicion' for a stop in the absence of traffic or equipment violations." "In order to effectuate a valid traffic stop, a police officer must have an articulable and reasonable suspicion that a vehicle or one of its occupants is subject to seizure for a violation of law."

What is not allowed in Michigan is a pretext stop of a motor vehicle. This means the police officer pulled over the driver, because she was driving a red jeep, or the officer pulled over the driver, because of their race or national origin. A police officer in reality would never admit to it, but equally, the cop can't say "well I had a hunch the driver was drunk" or "they just left a bar, and I pulled them over". If we have a case where the cop is relying on assumptions (leaving a bar) rather than actual observation (ran a red light) to make the stop, we have a defense to your DUI case.

I file motions all the time on DUI cases in Michigan when there is no evidence that the traffic code was violated, and the officer had no legal reason for conducting the stop. I see a lot of officers that put the "reason" in their police report, but a quick review of the available video or audio indicate that the police report is not accurate on that account.

Officers don't typically tell the driver every reason why they pulled them over, or even put it in their police report, because they want to keep it as vague as possible in case they need to embellish a bit later on. I purposely lock police officers into their police reports so they cannot reach for extra reasons for the stop. Here is an example

Me: Officer, before we proceed, I would like you to take a look at your police report, and let myself and the court know if there is anything you would like to add to the report at this time

Officer: It looks good to me

Me: Ok, I just want to be sure. I know you are a detailed officer who keeps good records, and documents any and all-important facts and observations, so are you sure you would not like to add something?

Officer: No, I am good.

Me: Officer, you stated on direct that you pulled my client over for not using a turn signal as they turned left onto Grand River Avenue, is that an accurate statement?

Officer: Yes

Me: Is not it also true that you made this observation from about 300 feet away at night with heavy rain and multiple vehicles in the area.

Officer: I saw what I saw

Me: Officer, I would like to you to take a moment to watch the in-car dash camera on the incident, and what I believe to be the moment where my client made that turn. (video reveals that due to the weather conditions, time of night and distance that it is not clear if a turn signal was used)

Officer: I saw what I saw, and it does not matter, because I then caught him speeding and weaving in and out of lanes.

Me: Officer, show me where in your police report it indicates my client was either speeding or weaving.

Officer: Well I did not put it in there

Me: Officer, I gave you two chances to amend you report, to add all the relevant and important facts into the report, and you did not do so.

Officer: I forgot about those until now

While the judge will still weigh the new "reasons" for the traffic stop as part of his/her decision, we've hurt the officer's credibility in that they are now only adding these new set of facts after their original facts were at least partially called into question. The officer only added in facts when they were desperate, and we have locked the officer into his police report at the beginning, and when they undoubtedly make these additions, it is easier to argue lack of credibility.

In contrast, I get cases where it's quite obvious that the police officer pulled over the car, because they suspected a drunk driver or they simply pulled the car over because they wanted to; as long as a traffic violation was committed, the real reason no longer matters.

Another way a police officer can pull someone over without observing a violation is by running the license plate of that vehicle to see the status of the registration and insurance, and the officer can assume the registered owner is the one driving the same vehicle, which happens if the registered owner has a warrant for their arrest, and an officer stumbles upon that car and runs the license plate.

Officers like to get creative when they want to pull over a vehicle and may cite a dangling object in the rearview mirror, or a trailer hitch, or even a license plate cover blocking access to the registration sticker. All these reasons have been challenged by me, and other lawyers in courts around Michigan, and are fact specific, with cases going either way on motions for dismissal.

If you've been charged with a DUI in Michigan, and you disagree with the reason provided by the officer in his police report, such as running a red light or not using a turn signal to turn or switch lanes then we're going to file a motion in pursuit of a ruling for an illegal stop, and for the evidence to be suppressed. If there is no physical evidence such as a video to back us up, the argument has a steeper hill to climb, as it is the officer's credibility on the stand, but in my experience if the officer is lying about the traffic stop, he/she is likely lying about other things, and if we can put their credibility into question then we may be able to sway a judge to grant our motion to suppress on this type of issue.

(15) CHALLENGING THE STOP: CHALLENGING THE 911 TIPSTER

I handle several DUI cases each year, which originate with a 911 call placed by an eyewitness to the police department. These calls are made by other drivers, pedestrians and sometimes pranksters. The one thing they have in common is they are usually referred to as anonymous tips. Sometimes we have an actual physical known witness, but that is quite rare. These "tips" result in several traffic stops, usually without additional direct officer observation of driving or even a traffic code violation.

Michigan law says that an anonymous tip by itself cannot create the reasonable suspicion necessary for a *Terry* stop, but if the officers see for themselves that part of the information in an anonymous tip is true, then the officers may reasonably rely on it. The court standard is known as totality of the circumstances.

For example, if someone calls 911 and reports a red pickup truck driving crazy on I-75, but extraordinarily little additional information, it is unlikely the police can just pull over the first red pickup truck they see on I-75. The Court is looking for adequate indicia of reliability. Nothing prevents them from making the stop, but if fruits of a crime are discovered or suspicion of a DUI offense comes from the stop, then a motion to dismiss should be filed immediately.

This same red pickup truck has a better argument for being pulled over if the caller also provided a license plate number, the make and model, possibly a description of the driver or any other specific facts about poor driving, and the officer can confirm these facts. There is no right or wrong amount of additional information; each set of facts will dictate a different evaluation. Further, if the cops show up on I-75 and spots a red pickup truck, and he sees the driver commit a traffic violation, it no longer matters what the 911 call says, because they have an independent reason to pull the truck over.

The Michigan Supreme Court has previously ruled that citizen-informants reporting suspicious activities that they have personally observed should be deemed inherently reliable "when the information is sufficiently detailed and is corroborated within a reasonable period of time by the cops own observations."

Anytime a 911 call is the basis of a traffic stop for a DUI case, it is important to begin with the source of the information. Listening to the 911 call, and any subsequent dispatch recordings or logs. It is a viable defense to challenge a traffic stop when the police officer lacks independent reasoning for conducting the stop.

This is a good situation to lock the officer into his police report and get him to admit that he himself did not observe any traffic violations, but rather relied on the 911 tipster information. He may say he verified the license plate or the general area where the car was, but this is ripe for challenge. If the officer observed his own reasons, the evaluation would be outside the scope of the 911 tipster defense theory. If he did not, then we need to lock him into this story, because we can then focus our efforts on discrediting what the caller said and relying on the caller's observations.

Here is an example of how my client would challenge their case with a 911 tipster involved. Let's assume that someone calls 911 on my client and reports that my client is driving a red pickup truck and going in and out of lanes, and the caller says my client is driving drunk; they provide the streets where they saw the driving, and the direction the truck is headed.

First, we need to assess whether this is an anonymous caller or was a name and other information provided. If witness information is available then they would likely be a witness for the prosecution, and they would be cross-examined about their observations.

If the caller is truly anonymous then a motion to dismiss would be viable without confirmation by the police. This would mean that when the officer found the red pickup truck, the truck was complying with the law, and the only reason for the traffic stop was the information from the call. We could argue that the caller was wrong, lying, mistaken or simply this is a different red truck. No matter the truth, the burden is on the prosecutor here.

We would argue that based on the totality of the circumstances, even if a license plate is confirmed or some other information, that absent the corroboration of the poor driving or traffic violations, the stop was illegal, and any evidence thereafter should be seized.

This argument has been a winner before in Michigan courts, in the *People v Barbarich* case, the Court stated that "an uncorroborated tip emanating from an unidentifiable source lacking any pertinent detail and suggesting only an ordinary traffic violation" did not justify the warrantless search and seizure.

The argument is that the law cannot allow any prankster or disgruntled driver to initiate a seizure of another motor vehicle without an officer's confirmation. Drivers have the right to be left alone and cannot be harassed on the road absent a valid reason to be seized in their cars.

This type of motion really comes down to the facts of your case, and the judge hearing the motion. It can go either way, but this type of challenge is always worth the effort, because your case can be dismissed on the spot without the risk of trial.

(16) & (17) CHALLENGING THE STOP: THE SLEEPING OPERATOR - CAR NOT IN MOTION

Most people imagine a DUI case involving a moving vehicle with a police officer putting on their sirens and lights and pulling that driver over. Occasionally a client of mine is not even awake when approached by the police; this is the sleeping operator defense.

Current case law states that a person sleeping in a motionless car cannot be held to be operating, and therefore cannot be convicted of drunk driving. The key to this law is the "motionless" aspect. The court does not end their analysis once they see a sleeping driver, the court is also looking for evidence that the vehicle had previously been in motion or could go into motion in its current state. Without present operation, the prosecution must piece back the past to show the element of operation.

There is plenty of cases where driver's pass out at a drive-thru or at a red light with their foot on the break. This is evidence that the driver WAS operating before passing out, and at any moment the car can go into motion if their foot leaves the break. The court looks at the danger that the car poses, and if the car can be put into motion because of a significant risk of causing collision or damage to property; operation does not end until the car is returned to a position that no longer poses this risk.

When I evaluate a case with a client who tells me they were passed out at the wheel, we're looking for where the car was located when the police arrived, and if the ignition is on, and if the car is in park or not. We are also looking for signs that the prosecution can show that at "some point before" the police arrived to find the sleeping operator, the car was in motion.

In a sleeping operator case, I typically file a motion to dismiss for two reasons. One, it creates potential leverage to work out a great deal, and two if we have the right facts, it may lead to a dismissal of charges. We are looking for facts where the engine is off; that is ideal, but not typical. If we have a case where the engine is on, and my client is "sleeping it off", we are hoping that the car is in park. If we have those facts, we still need to overcome the circumstantial evidence that a prosecutor may present to show prior operation.

It is important to put together a timeline; the longer the car has been sitting there unbothered by the police, the better for the case. The prosecutor has the burden to show the driver HAD operated that vehicle either impaired or intoxicated by law. As time goes by, the field sobriety tests, and BAC readings become a lot less reliable for the prosecution's case.

(18) CHALLENGING THE STOP: USING THE DISPATCH LOGS

Most attorneys overlook dispatch logs when examining their client's case. While most DUI cases involve an officer already out on patrol or on the lookout for possible drunk drivers, a portion of DUI cases involve accidents and 911 tipsters calling in about incidents.

When I am working on one of these types of cases, I order the dispatch logs and 911 call to learn more about what led up to the police arriving at the scene of the incident. A review of these records is invaluable, which allows us to establish a timeline, and hear exactly what the caller stated to the 911 operator. This information will allow us to know what the officer knew when he was arriving at the scene of an accident or on the look-out for a car.

When I listen to dispatch records and read the logs, I am looking for details such as make and model, license plate numbers, specific facts about driving, locations and descriptions of occupants of a vehicle.

Dispatch records may contain possible admissions by my client in a situation where my client or someone who was with them calls into 911, and states so and so was driving and crashed. This information could be used against my client to prove operation at trial. Better to know these facts immediately when sorting through my client's options.

(19) CHALLENGING THE ARREST PRELIMINARY BREATH TEST (PBT)

Most DUI cases in Michigan have multiple BAC readings. The first reading typically comes at the scene of the crime in the form of preliminary breath test. Officers offer this test in order to assist in justifying their arrest. The defendant has the option to take the test, or decline; if you decline, it is a 2-point civil infraction (if under 21). In the end, this infraction is usually dismissed anyway as part of an agreement that is worked out with the prosecutor.

Police officers aren't always clear about the consequences of not taking the test, and are ok with my client believing that a refusal of the PBT will lead to loss of license, and 6 points on their license, which is not true (these sanctions apply to the Datamaster).

I typically believe taking the test only hurts your case, because if you blow over the limit, and there is evidence of driving, the officer has a slam dunk case for a legal arrest. Without the test, an officer must rely on his subjective observations, and if you decline field sobriety tests, then the officer really must stretch his rationale, and we stand a great chance to challenge the arrest.

In Michigan, a police officer may arrest a person based in whole or in part on PBT results. Once used as part of the arrest, the test is typically no longer admissible with limited exceptions.

So, the first part of beating the PBT is to not take it at all. I have filed a lot of motions to challenge an arrest, because the cop did not have a PBT result as part of his arrest; we were able to attack field sobriety tests and officer observations and beat the arrest.

If a PBT is administered, the question becomes, do we want to try to use the results to help or case, or make sure to keep it out of the case. Most would say, let us keep it out, because it is evidence against me. Here is how I have used the PBT to help my clients win at trial.

Let us assume my client is charged with a High BAC/Super Drunk offense in Michigan. We have a PBT result of say 0.13, we then have a Datamaster result of 0.18 an hour later. How can that benefit my client? Well a High BAC prosecution requires that the prosecutor prove beyond a reasonable doubt that when my client was driving his/her car, their BAC was over 0.17. Well alcohol levels go up and down after your last drink. The question is, when the police stop you, are you rising or falling in your BAC level?

With these two readings, we have a clear rise in BAC level. This would assist in an argument that my client's BAC was rising, and likely was below 0.17, and closer to the 0.13 result at the scene. This type of scenario has helped me resolve cases with very favorable plea deals, especially in certain counties that never bargain on Super Drunk cases.

We also use these numbers at trial, but in order to introduce the PBT at trial, we need to fit it into one of the three exceptions to the rule. The three exceptions in Michigan are the following:

1. The test results may be admitted assisting the court or hearing officer in determining a challenge to the validity of an arrest. MCL 257.625a(2)(b)(i).
2. At trial, the defendant may offer the PBT result as evidence of his or her BrAC to rebut testimony elicited on cross-examination of a defense witness that the defendant's BrAC was higher at the time of the charged offense than when a chemical test was administered. MCL 257.625a(2)(b)(ii).
3. At trial, the prosecution may introduce PBT results as evidence of the defendant's BrAC only to rebut testimony elicited on cross-examination of a prosecution witness that is offered or elicited to prove that the defendant's BrAC was lower at the time of the charged offense than when the chemical test was later administered (the rising blood or breath alcohol content defense). MCL 257.625a(2)(b)(iii).

In order to get the PBT into our case, I would go for the second exception. While it would not be automatically admitted, a crafty cross-examination of the DataMaster operator is likely to be fruitful.

With the right judge, it is also possible to sneak the result in through the prosecution's witness, and most judges in my experience would view the matter as a matter of fairness; if there's another BAC reading out there that might assist the trier of fact (the jury), they may let it in, and let the jury decide what to do with it.

The PBT is not automatically admissible because it is simply not as reliable as the Datamaster, which is tested, calibrated and checked on a regular basis (weekly and every 120 days). Many PBT devices go long periods of time without calibrating and could sit in cold or hot weather for long periods of time. The key is identifying the result, and how to use it to your advantage.

(20) Challenging the Arrest Statements/Miranda Issues

When I handle a DUI case in Michigan, the first thing I look for is operation. You cannot have a drunk driving case without some driving. Most cases begin with an officer conducting a traffic stop where the operation is clear, and not contested. If my client's driving is not as straightforward then I am looking for the evidence that the prosecution will use to show he/she was the driver.

In this situation, the evidence usually comes right from my client's mouth. It is usually too late to swallow these words once charged, but in the right situation, we may be able to suppress these incriminating statements.

As a prosecutor and defense lawyer, I have handled cases where there is no eyewitness to driving, and the defendant makes no such admissions about driving. That missing fact usually helps lead to a very favorable plea deal, or a strong defense at trial.

Hearsay does not apply to the charged defendant in Michigan. A police officer can take the stand and testify that the defendant admitted to driving. In respect to that, the 5th Amendment protects the defendant from making any admissions, but most are voluntary without knowledge of the ramifications.

This situation pops up a lot with my clients. My client tells me that they were not read their *Miranda* rights. They wonder if this alone could lead to a dismissal, and the answer is generally no. It may not even be required in the case depending on when the statements were made.

When you are pulled over by a police officer, or an officer pulls up alongside an accident, the officer can ask questions to get information. Let us assume my client is standing outside of his car with two friends when the police arrive. At this point there is no direct evidence of who was driving but rather only circumstantial evidence.

The cop says to my client, where were you coming from? My client answers. The cop says, how did you hit the guardrail? My client answers. At this point, my client has admitted to driving. These statements are likely to be admissible because they are not made during a custodial interrogation.

In Michigan, a Custodial interrogation means questioning instigated by the police while a person is in custody, not necessarily arrested but not free to leave. Conversations while sitting inside your own car or standing outside the vehicle are not in custody. There has even case law that says when you are sitting in a police car for "protection" or to get out of the bad weather, you are not in custody.

Whether a defendant is in custody for the purposes of *Miranda* is determined by considering the totality of the circumstances and asking whether a reasonable person in the defendant's position would feel free to leave.

Statements made that are not in response to police questioning are not subject to the protection of *Miranda.* Statements that fall into this category are spontaneous utterances, statements that are nonresponsive to the question asked, and volunteered statements made not in response to any question.

Along with statements about driving, statements about drinking, leaving a bar, feeling intoxicated and other incriminating statements are usually admissible. So, what sort of technique or strategy do I use when it comes to statements?

I am looking for a situation where the police arrive, and my client does not admit to driving. He either does not say anything or denies it. The police will become frustrated and continue asking my client. As this goes on, they will likely start pushing for PBT's, field sobriety tests, threatening an arrest and other signs of authority. At some point this struggle steps over the line, and my client in my view is now not feeling the freedom to leave and is in custody. Hopefully, my client is smart enough to ask straight out: am I free to leave? If the cop says no, then we have a great argument to suppress any statements. A client should always force an officer to answer whether they are free to leave, because the officer will say no, and *Miranda* applies.

My client may or may not admit to driving at this point. If he does, then we move to suppress this statement, and let the case go forward without this piece of evidence. We can use this to have further field sobriety and chemical tests thrown out as well as challenge the basis of the arrest. Or, we can use this defense at trial, because the admission of driving may be suppressed, and operation cannot be proven to the necessary legal proof. Now there could be circumstantial evidence of driving, but at least we have knocked the most incriminating evidence out of the prosecutor's evidence.

The police can save themselves a lot of trouble by properly reading their *Miranda* warnings to the client, but most cops only associate the warnings when they place handcuffs on the client. If the client speaks post *Miranda* well the statements may then be admissible depending on the facts of the case.

(21) Challenging the Arrest

Field Sobriety Tests

When a client is pulled over by the police or investigated for a DUI at the scene of accident, the police are now in evidence gathering mode. They are looking for evidence of operation; once they have that, they are then looking for evidence of "being drunk". This second bucket of evidence comes from the preliminary breath tests, officer observations, statements by the defendant, and field sobriety tests.

A lot of attorneys overlook field sobriety tests and focus on trying to attack the chemical tests. While it is especially important to examine all your defenses with the chemical tests, the field sobriety tests can be extremely fruitful for a motion to suppress based on an illegal arrest or assist in a defense at trial.

When an officer makes the decision to arrest you, it is a combination of evidence of operation and probable cause that you committed a drunk driving offense. An officer offers up a PBT test along with numerous field sobriety tests; most people agree to both, which is a mistake. I have already discussed how to beat, and use the PBT in your favor, but field sobriety tests can also be declined.

Taking a series of field sobriety tests is very unlikely to help your case. The tests are usually taken at night, in potentially freezing weather with rain or snow falling, on the side of the road with other cars flying by and pressure from an authority figure. You are also likely tired and extremely nervous; it is like trying to tie your shoes while standing in the middle of a lion's cage.

If you do not take field sobriety tests, and you decline the PBT, then an officer may not have enough to make a legal arrest. An officer will have to rely on statements about drinking, how you walked, and talked and observations of your eyes, your smells and your demeanor. If you do not open your mouth or make admissions, then the prosecutor has a thin case for showing a valid arrest. It is very possible to move for suppression under these circumstances.

If my client took field sobriety tests, it's likely that they "failed" enough to justify an arrest; if a client happened to do very well on the tests then they can help in the argument that the officer lacked probable cause to arrest you, especially if there was not a PBT over the legal limit.

Field sobriety tests can also assist at trial. Each test has a set of specific instructions. If an officer fails to read those instructions properly then the test results should be thrown out. If an officer misrepresents how my client performed in his police report, because the video shows the client doing better than documented, it could hurt the officer's credibility on the entire case.

An officer is trained by the National Highway Traffic Safety Administration, and these standards are available to the public. I use the same manual to attack the officer's administration of the tests, and their selection of those tests. For example, an officer is trained that there are only three field sobriety tests that have been deemed scientifically reliable to detect intoxication/impairment.

Horizontal Gaze Nystagmus (HGN) is one of three standard field sobriety exercises conducted by law enforcement. This test looks for involuntary jerking of your eyes as you gaze toward the sides. The other two tests are the walk-and-turn and the one-leg stand. Any test outside of these three should NOT be used. If an officer conducts anything else then they are conducting themselves outside of their training, and it opens the door for an attack on multiple fronts.

Finally, if we're working with BAC levels that straddle the 0.08 or 0.17 lines for different charges, a strong performance on the field sobriety tests can sway a jury to go with our argument that the BAC reading is inflated, and not accurate as to what it was when my client was driving the car. Here is an example.

My client is charged with an OWI. He is stopped at 2 am by the police. My client refuses the PBT, but takes field sobriety tests, which he does well on. The officer admits to him passing most of the tests, and the video backs this up, and even discredits some of the officers' observations as being too bearish. The client has a 0.10 BAC at 3 am. At this point we can argue rising blood.

The theory goes: look how well the client did on the field sobriety tests, that does not look like someone over the legal limit. Yes, he blew a 0.10 an hour later, but he had just finished drinks before getting in his car, and when driving he was below 0.08, and it only rose to 0.10 after time has passed. This technique requires some well-planned cross-examination of the police officers, and potentially the Michigan State Police representative or an expert witness brought in by the defense.

(22) CHALLENGING THE ARREST OFFICER OUTSIDE OF JURISDICTION

When a client is arrested for drunk driving it Michigan, we either see the Michigan State Police, a local sheriff's department or a local city or township government making the arrest. Some cases have multiple police agencies involved. The question becomes, what power does a police agency have to make an arrest? Here are some general guidelines for Michigan, and how certain situations could open the possibility for a motion for an illegal arrest.

In Michigan, a police officer can make an arrest outside of its jurisdiction if they are enforcing the state laws along with the Michigan State Police or with a local police agency of that area. For example, a Novi police officer can operate outside of Novi if they are working with the Michigan State Police or can operate in the City of Northville if working with that agency.

Police officers may also act outside their jurisdiction if they witness a violation of the law inside of their own jurisdiction. So, with this example, the same Novi officer witnesses someone speeding in Novi, and they drive into Northville Township; the officer can continue to pursue and make a stop and an arrest.

The issue comes when a police officer is outside their jurisdiction to begin with, and at that point pull someone over. If this were to be the case for one of my client's, we would file a motion moving for a dismissal of charges due to an illegal arrest and seizure by the police officer. We would move to have any evidence suppressed as well.

The only way this last situation could be allowed is if the officer witnesses a felony in their presence. If a prosecutor tried to charge my client with a third offense felony DUI after this sort of stop, I would still file a motion, because at the time of the stop/pursuit, the officer has no reason to believe the driver has prior offenses, and THIS one could be a felony. If the officer claims the offense were fleeing and eluding, which is a felony, this would be a better reason for the stop, and might hold up in court.

(23) CHALLENGING FIELD SOBRIETY

TESTS HORIZONTAL GAZE NYSTAGMUS

One of the most common field sobriety tests requested by police officers in Michigan is the HGN test. Nystagmus is an involuntary twitching of the eyes. When an officer checks your eyes, he is looking for this switching. The officer is looking for distinct Nystagmus at the maximum deviation, a lack of smooth pursuit and the onset of the Nystagmus prior to 45 degrees. The proper methods for administering the HGN test is laid out in detail in the National Highway Traffic Safety Administration (NHTSA) manual.

This is the most popular test offered, and many officers and prosecutors believe this test to be the holy grail of field sobriety tests. While the test does have some scientific importance, the test is only reliable if conducted properly. When I review the police reports and videos in a DUI case, I am looking to make sure the officer followed all the proper instructions and all precautions were taken to have a fair test for my client.

The test begins with the officer instructing the client to put their feet together and keep their hands to their side. The officer will then instruct the client to follow a finger, pen or other device with your eyes, and making sure to keep your head from moving. It is important to make sure that the officer has asked the client about contact lenses, and any other medical conditions that might be relevant.

Before examining your eyes for the three above factors, the officer should be checking for equal tracking and to make sure your pupils are of the same size; failure to do so, and failure to properly ask about contact lenses could deem the results unreliable.

The officer checks for equal tracking by starting at the nose and going right then back to the center then left. Without this initial check, the rest of the exam is worthless.

Once the officer has conducted this trial run, he is now looking for smooth pursuit, and looking to see if there is involuntary jerking of the eyes as the object goes from side to side; this is supposed to be two full passes. The officer then looks for Nystagmus at maximum deviation meaning that there is no white visible at the outside of the eye; it requires the officer to hold your eye at maximum deviation for at least 4 seconds, or the results could be unreliable.

Finally, the officer will now look for onset of Nystagmus prior to 45 degrees, and vertical Nystagmus. The first requires the officer to bring the eye out from the middle slowly, and to look for the angle of the onset to see if it is prior to 45 degrees. The second requires the officer to move your eye vertically, and to evaluate the onset of Nystagmus.

Failure to follow ANY of these vital instructions could cause Nystagmus, which would otherwise not be present, and will give a false result. The officer's goal is to find Nystagmus, which in his training tells him that the driver is intoxicated or impaired, which helps prosecute the case. It is quite rare that the dash cam video provides a full account of this test to ensure that the proper technique and instructions were provided

When I look at the evidence in a DUI case, I carefully evaluate any information available to see if the HGN test was done properly. If there is no video then I am going to cross-examine the officer on all the instructions which are laid out in his training manual, and to make sure he followed it. The officer may or may not have followed it, but usually if an officer is not telling the truth, something will pop up during a carefully tailored cross-examination.

Usually the most fruitful result of this cross-examination is evidence that my client was facing headlights or traffic, which is not allowed per the training manual for a proper HGN test. Putting the HGN test in question may not be the smoking gun to a not guilty verdict, but it can be a further minor victory when it comes to the officer's credibility and attention to detail, which puts other parts of the case into question.

(24) CHALLENGING FIELD SOBRIETY TESTS ONE-LEG-STAND

Along with the HGN test, the next most popular field sobriety test in Michigan is the one-leg-stand. Like the HGN, the test must be properly administered for it mean anything for the prosecution, and as a piece to the puzzle of deciding intoxication and/or impairment.

If the defense does not rigorously evaluate and challenge the procedure and the instructions then it does not matter, because the results are the only thing that a judge or jury will see.

The instructions for the one-leg-stand are awfully specific and listed in the National Highway Traffic Safety Administration (NHTSA) manual. Here are the instructions, which must be adhered to for a proper test:

#1 - Stand straight and put your feet together

#2 - Keep your arms at your side

#3 - Stay this way until told otherwise

At this point the officer must ask the participant if they understand. If the participant says they understand then the officer will continue:

#4 - Please raise one leg, it can be either leg

#5 - Keep your leg 6 inches off the ground, and point your foot out

#6 - Keep both of your legs straight and your eyes on the elevated foot

#7 - The officer will then have the participant count 1001, 1002, 1003 and so forth until told to stop.

The officer should administer this entire instructional and balancing/counting in thirty seconds. The NHTSA manual instructs the officer to look for the following clues for impairment:

If the participant sways, uses arms to balance, hops and/or puts his/her foot down. If the participant cannot perform the test, then you are marked down for showing signs of all four.

Most of the time, the officer does not administer this test correctly. The conditions of the road may not match what is required (flat/even surface among others), he may not have given the proper instructions or used the proper thirty second timeframe.

Most defense attorneys do not even bother to review the videos and scrutinize the officer reports enough to realize this, and if they do, they need to know what to do with it.

Like the HGN, a false positive test may not be the smoking gun, but it is piece of the puzzle of shining light on the prosecution's inconsistent and questionable case. If the defense can show that a few of the field sobriety tests are not reliable, and can show any cracks in the officer's credibility who improperly administered the exams, then it's a big win for giving the jury something to hold their hat on when it comes to finding reasonable doubt.

(25) CHALLENGING FIELD SOBRIETY

TESTS WALK AND TURN

When it comes to public perception of drunk driving cases in Michigan, most people imagine the accused performing the walk and turn on the side of the road. The walk and turn has become so well known, because it's used in the media as a way to show someone pulled over and under investigation, and that perception is reality in Michigan; the walk and turn is a major part of an officer's toolbox for a DUI investigation.

Like the other field sobriety tests, this test must be properly administered and has two different parts: proper instructions to the participant and the performance stage. Here are the instructions which must be provided to the participant for the test to be properly conducted, and all of them must be demonstrated by the officer to the participant.

#1 - Place your left foot on the line (the officer must demonstrate this)
#2 - Place your right foot in front of your left foot, with the heel of your right foot against the toe of your left foot
#3- Keep your arms down at your sides
#4 - Only begin when told to do so

The officer will then ask the participant if they understand the instructions. The participant must say YES, if not, the officer must clarify anything asked by the participant.

If the participant says YES, then the officer will instruct the participant to walk nine steps heel to toe forward, turn while keeping your lead foot on the line, and take several small steps with the other foot before walking back nine heel to toe steps. Along with these instructions the officer must demonstrate it for the participant. Along with these steps, the participant must look at their feet, keep their arms down at their sides and count while walking.

Frankly, this is a lot to remember and a stressful situation for the participant. Despite the odds against the participant to perform this accurately, the NHTSA tells the officer to look for 8 clues for intoxication and/or impairment. If you show 2 signs, you fail the test according to their rule book. Here are the 8 clues:

Cannot balance during instructions, starts too soon, stops while walking, fails to touch heel to toe, stepping off the line, uses arms for balance, improper turn and wrong number of steps.

If the participant cannot perform the test, then you fail all 8 parts. When I evaluate a field sobriety test as part of a DUI Case, I am looking for an officer who gives incorrect instructions, does not demonstrate the test and orders the wrong number of steps. We are also looking for what the NHTSA manual calls proper conditions.

If the officer does not do his job properly then the test results lose credibility, and I would use to paint doubt on the prosecution's entire case. If there is one crack, one error, one point of unfairness to my client then the whole case likely has issues.

(26) CHALLENGING FIELD SOBRIETY

TESTS NUMBERS AND ALPHABET

The three above field sobriety tests are the only ones listed in the NHSTA manual, and officers are instructed to stick to those three tests, and those three tests alone.

In Michigan, these "well-trained" officers do not follow their own rule book. In most of the cases that I handle, an officer has my client sing the alphabet, count backwards or estimate time. These are improper tests and should not be used in Michigan. If an officer uses them, I am going to go after him for not following the rules and trying to "get" my client by playing outside of the rules. If an officer cannot follow their own protocol, which they are trained on when it comes to field sobriety tests, then what else did they do incorrectly?

I do not even bother to challenge these extra field sobriety tests, because they are not part of the rule book, and outside the officer's protocol. My client does not get a say in the rules or the standards set, so when the police and prosecution make the rules, they better sure follow them. You cannot change the rules because you are lazy or do not know how to instruct and/or administer the proper field sobriety tests.

(27 TO 30) MICHIGAN IMPLIED CONSENT

In Michigan, when you operate a motor vehicle, you consent to certain rules. The rule book in Michigan, specifically under 2014 PA 315, provides that a person who operates a motor vehicle on a public highway or other place open to the general public or generally accessible to motor vehicles within this state, including an area designated for the parking of vehicles, is considered to have given consent to chemical tests of his or her blood, breath, or urine to determine the amount of alcohol, controlled substance, or another intoxicating substance, or any combination of them, if the person is arrested for one of the enumerated crimes in the statute, including the principal drunk driving offenses along with several other major driving offenses, and the officer has reasonable grounds to believe the driver was operating a vehicle in violation of section 625 of the Michigan Vehicle Code.

What does all that mean? It means when you drive and you refuse you provide a chemical test sample, the officer can seek a warrant and force you to provide a sample, which is typically a blood draw at the hospital. This law is in place so people cannot escape providing important evidence in their DUI case; without a chemical test, prosecutions of drunk driving cases would be a lot less effective.

If arrested for a DUI in Michigan, the officer must read the Defendant his/her chemical test rights and be asked to take a chemical test; this test can be blood, breath or urine. This test can look for alcohol, drugs or both. Along with this mandated test, the Defendant may request his/her own test.

If the Defendant refuses the test, they will be forced to have blood drawn via court order and have an automatic one-year suspension of their driver's license along with six points added to their driving record. This happens no matter the outcome of the criminal case.

The Secretary of State has their own power to do this to your license merely based on the refusal. The only way to possibly prevent this suspension is by requesting an implied consent hearing within 14 days.

The necessary information and form are attached to the temporary license provided by the police officer at the time of release from jail. The officer will be subpoenaed to this hearing where the hearing officer will evaluate four issues; the rules of evidence do not apply, and the criminal standard of reasonable doubt is not in place.

Here are the four issues which can be explored at this hearing. You only need to win on one to win the hearing. Anytime a client finds themselves in this position we file the hearing request and prepare to win. Unfortunately, many clients contact me when it is too late, and do not realize the consequences of the situation.

(a) Whether the peace officer had reasonable grounds to believe that the person had committed a crime described in [MCL 257.625c(1)].

(b) Whether the person was placed under arrest for a crime described in [MCL 257.625c(1)].

(c) If the person refused to submit to the test upon the request of the officer, whether the refusal was reasonable.

(d) Whether the person was advised of the rights under [MCL 257.625a(6)].

The burden is on the police officer to show compliance with all four issues. While that appears to be a favorable occurrence, the standard of proof is a lot lower than criminal cases. The standard of proof at the hearing is a preponderance of the evidence (51 vs 49 percent). If the officer does not show within 20 minutes of the scheduled time, the matter is dismissed; if the client does not show, the suspension goes into place on default.

So how do I approach implied consent hearings? Well the first part is obtaining all the evidence; the videos, audio, dispatch, police reports, accident reports etc. Sometimes an implied consent hearing happens before a client is even charged, because blood was drawn, which could take months to get results for the prosecutor to charge with, but the Secretary of State goes forward with the hearing. We are looking to attack all four issues if possible, but typically you are lucky to find an issue with one rather than all four.

The first issue is "whether the peace officer had reasonable grounds to believe that the person had committed a crime described in" MCL 257.625c(1) of the Michigan Vehicle Code. This does not mean a crime had to be committed, but rather than officer had a reasonable believe that one had been committed, a pretty low standard.

Typically, the officer will provide enough testimony to win on this issue. One situation where my client can win on this issue is if the officer had truly little to base his arrest on. If the officer's testimony is thin, there is a chance of prevailing on this issue, but it is usually not the most fruitful.

The second issue that the police officer must prove at an implied consent hearing is that the person was placed under arrest for one of the crimes specified in MCL 257.625c(1). What I am looking for on this issue is the officer to testify to the crime of arrest; simply stating an arrest was made is not enough, because there are many reasons to arrest that are not under the implied consent law.

If you are arrested for reckless driving this is not under the implied consent law. Further, the person who refuses the chemical test must be under arrest when asked; if they are not yet under arrest then the law does not apply. This situation is possible to identify by watching the videos and listening to the audio. Further, the arrest must be valid; if through cross-examination we can exploit an illegal arrest, a client can prevail on this issue.

The statute states that the third issue that must be proved at an implied consent hearing is if the person refused to submit to the test upon the request of the officer, whether the refusal was reasonable." MCL 257.625f(4)(c).

This is fact specific and could involve someone outright refusing or someone who attempts to take the test, but either the machine or the operator determines that the Defendant is not making a sincere effort to blow into the machine. An interesting situation arises when a client refuses but shortly thereafter says they will indeed take the test.

Most officers will allow it as it is a lot easier to do a breath test vs going to a hospital for a blood test and to acquire a warrant in the middle of the night from a judge. This is called curing the refusal and the hearing officer will hear all sides of the story to determine the reasonableness of the refusal if the officer does not allow the curing.

Some common themes that arise with the third is choice of test. Under current Michigan law, the Defendant cannot choose which test to take. So, if a Defendant says, yes, I agree, but I will only take a urine test, that will be a refusal if the officer wants to do blood or breath. The choice is with the officer only. Another theme is right to counsel; Michigan courts have long held that the defendant has no right to counsel before or during a police-administered chemical test inasmuch as the testing procedure is not considered a critical stage in the criminal proceedings.

Although this seems like a closed issue; courts have said that if a

Defendant requests to call a lawyer as long as it's a reasonable request and does not delay the process, a phone call is allowed; if that is denied then the refusal may not be reasonable and the case can be tossed out. Ultimately, the issue is whether the driver's refusal was reasonable based on the totality of circumstances existing at the time of the refusal.

If a client has hemophilia, diabetes or a condition requiring the use of an anticoagulant under the direction of a doctor then the Defendant does not need to consent to the withdrawal of blood. It would be reasonable under the law for this person to refuse, and the sanctions would not apply.

The fourth and last issue the police must prove at an implied consent hearing is that the Defendant was advised of the chemical test rights stated in MCL 257.625a(6)(b), which provides that a person arrested for one of the crimes enumerated in MCL 257.625c(1) must be advised of all of the following:

(i) If he or she takes a chemical test of his or her blood, urine, or breath administered at the request of a peace officer, he or she has the right to demand that a person of his or her own choosing administer 1 of the chemical tests.

(ii) The results of the test are admissible in a judicial proceeding as provided under this act and will be considered with other admissible evidence in determining the defendant's innocence or guilt.

(iii) He or she is responsible for obtaining a chemical analysis of a test sample obtained at his or her own request.

(iv) If he or she refuses the request of a peace officer to take a test described in subparagraph (i), a test shall not be given without a court order, but the peace officer may seek to obtain a court order.

(v) Refusing a peace officer's request to take a test described in subparagraph (i) will result in the suspension of his or her operator's or chauffeur's license and vehicle group designation or operating privilege and in the addition of 6 points to his or her driver record.

These instructions are listed on the back of the Officer's Report of Refusal to Submit to Chemical Test and Michigan Temporary Driving Permit, which is handed to you. An officer will typically read it word for word and let you look at it; the officer will usually put his initials on the paperwork to indicate it was read. When I am reviewing this issue, I review the form itself, and the audio and video, which may have recorded the reading of the rights.

What I am looking for in this situation is for the video or audio to show that the instructions were not read properly or the conversation between my client and the police officer contained inconsistent or improper information.

Sometimes a Defendant asks for additional information or advice; the officer is trained to not engage in these requests, and just stick to the script, but many officers do not do that. If the officer says the wrong thing or misleads or confuses my client outside the chemical test rights, then we may have a winner on issue four.

(31) HARDSHIP LICENSE 101

When a client hires me to work on their DUI case, and there is an implied consent issue, we always discuss the backup plan of a circuit court appeal for a hardship license. Many times, the circuit court appeal stands a better chance at saving my client's license than winning at the implied consent hearing.

The circuit court appeal happens after a decision is made on the implied consent hearing; this must happen within 63 days after the order of suspension is entered. The time can go beyond this with showing of good cause (up to 182 days).

The petition must be made in the circuit court of the county of arrest, and you are only eligible on your first implied consent refusal. The standard to receive a hardship license is "hardship". The petitioner must show why not having the ability to drive is impacting their job, school or other obligations. There cannot be an alternative option, hence the hardship, such as someone else to drive you.

I will have a client put together a comprehensive work or school schedule with maps and directions. We will research bus routes, cab fares and Uber fares. The goal is to show that driving to work is the only option, and there is no family member, friend or co-worker to assist. It would be a financial hardship and/or a huge time hardship to take cabs or public transportation.

Along with showing the hardship, my clients are already in counseling, going to AA, alcohol and drug testing and participating in community service. We need to show that if a judge is going to restore driving privileges that you are not a threat on the road, and you have everything under control.

The first step is filing the petition with supporting evidence of the above proactive steps and transportation documentation. We then attend the court hearing where the Secretary of State can send a representative.

If handled directly, I can usually sit down with the Secretary of State person and stipulate to granting the hardship license. This means we no longer need to convince the judge, and most judges will defer to the two parties. Every time, but one time I was able to convince the Secretary of State representative to sign off on an order before the hearing. The one time that did not happen, the representative did not show, and the judge granted it anyway.

From there we file the order with the Secretary of State and the new restricted license is granted and arrives in the mail soon after. This is how you win when it comes to hardship licenses in Michigan.

(32) SOBRIETY COURTS

In Michigan, sobriety courts are voluntary programs for a defendant to enter as part of a drunk driving case. Sobriety court is for repeat offenders or offenders with extremely high BAC levels. Defendants are not forced into sobriety court, but it is usually an alternative to jail time, and an opportunity to maintain your ability to drive when your license would otherwise be taken away.

When you enter sobriety court, you are committing yourself for 12 to 24 months of drug and alcohol testing, sometimes daily, and a total commitment to sobriety; violations will send you to jail for the maximum allotted penalty. Essentially, you are avoiding jail upfront, so if you mess up, you get the maximum.

If you enter a sobriety court which is approved by the State of Michigan, you could be eligible for a restricted driver's license, which you would otherwise not receive without sobriety court. For example, if you are convicted of a second DUI within 7 years, your license will be gone for a year; enter sobriety court, and you might be back on the road in 45-60 days.

Sobriety courts are a great option for a client who is seeking the available resources of the criminal justice system and are ready to embrace close supervision. The goal of the sobriety court is to reduce repeat offenses, get people sober, and head in the right direction.

Not all courts in Michigan have a sobriety court, and if they do, most require you to live within the jurisdiction of the court due to the need to supervise you when you are outside of the courtroom walls.

If my client is charged with a second offense DUI, or facing jail time for their case, and that court has sobriety case, then we put it on the table as a legitimate option. Because all my clients are proactive from day one, it is an easier transition into the sobriety court mindset. Both the client and the sobriety court must agree to begin a working relationship. A client must be deemed a "good candidate".

I have my clients screened and assessed early in the case by a substance abuse counselor, attend AA, participating in community service, alcohol and drug testing and engaged in substance abuse education. If my client selects sobriety court as their best path, we have already demonstrated a genuine desire to make changes, and head down the right path going forward. The interview and screening process goes a lot smoother when we have already checked off several boxes for the sobriety court team. Many times, my clients receive shorter stints in sobriety court, because they have been deemed to have made progress, which leads to obtaining a driver's license in a shorter period.

When jail and loss of license is on the table, sobriety court is a great option when the strengths outweigh the weaknesses of a client's case.

I have had clients save themselves months and years in jail, because together we put together a plan to earn a spot in sobriety court. The same clients who were going to lose their job, have to drop out of school, sell their homes and potentially lose their family were able to avoid that because they earned their license back by entering sobriety court. When a client of mine opts for sobriety court, I am extremely proud of them, because they know it will not be easy, but it is the best thing for them in both the short and long-term.

(33 & 34) VETERANS COURT & MENTAL HEALTH COURT

The State of Michigan is home to almost one million military veterans. Some of these veterans find themselves on the wrong side of the law. Some of these legal issues stem from service-related medical problems. In Michigan, a growing number of courts are now implementing Veterans Treatment Courts. These courts take the veteran outside of the typical criminal justice system, and place them in a more supportive environment, which coordinates and maximizes available resources and benefits to the veteran.

When I work with a new client, one of the questions I ask is if the client has any present involvement in the military, or anything in their past. If so, the next question is whether the court we are in has a Veterans Treatment Court, or if the court works with another court that has one. There are a few courts in Michigan, which allow a client to enter the Veterans Treatment Court of another district court.

If a client wishes to pursue a spot in a Veterans Court, then they will present their DD-214 form, which lists the service and discharge of the client. If my client does not have this form, we order the records from the National Personnel Records Center with the SF-180 form.

A Veterans Court offers a team approach like a sobriety court. It is geared toward misdemeanor offenses and can be considered a jail alternative; many of these offenses also involve substance abuse issues, which like the sobriety court, offer a comprehensive platform to deal with these issues with counseling, education and testing. What makes the Veterans Court different from sobriety court is the coordination of VA benefits such as treatment, medical help and housing. It is also a welcoming setting, which shows appreciation to the veteran for their service in conjunction with the present help from the court.

Along with Veterans Court, some courts have a Mental Health Treatment Court, which is open to everyone. The Mental Health Court can be a problem-solving court that offers therapeutic treatment for mental illnesses which lead to the offender breaking the law. Potential participants are recognized early by either their own attorney, the prosecutor or the judge.

The client is removed from the adversarial mainstream court process and placed in a community-based treatment setting, which looks to address underlying problems which lead to the criminal offense versus simple punishment. Along with mental health and substance abuse treatment, the mental health team connects participants with education, housing and jobs.

Instead of spending time in jail, and ignoring mental health issues, the real problems are tackled with the goal reducing recidivism and helping people get their life back on the right path.

(35) Discovery in Misdemeanor Cases

When I take on a new criminal misdemeanor, it is important to learn everything about my new client, but also to learn everything about the allegations that the client is facing. I call this the information gathering stage. Discovery is obtained through the police, prosecutor, outside agencies and private persons and businesses. Everything from the officer's police report to a surveillance video from a department store.

In Michigan, discovery in criminal cases is governed by MCR 6.201 and MCL 767.94a. Discovery can be conducted in Michigan via a discovery demand to the prosecution and police, the Freedom of Information Act (FOIA) or a subpoena to a witness for both testimony and/or physical evidence. It is important to be broad and expansive as possible; even if you are not sure an item exists (a video), it must be requested to be preserved and obtained or it can be destroyed as time goes on.

The process of obtaining discovery assists in identifying potential motions to file, trial defenses and creation of leverage for negotiation. Discovery obtained from these external sources is only half the story; my client, his/her witnesses and potential physical evidence is the other half of the equation. The defense team should hold the information advantage; the prosecutor has everything from the police department and agencies, but the defense has all of that plus their client's discovery.

Having both sides of the case is the key to leveraging the discovery process for use in pre-trial litigation, trial or brokering a deal. In a DUI case in Michigan, here are some common things we are looking to obtain:

1. Officer's police report
2. Client's driving record & criminal background
3. Field Sobriety tests
4. Datamaster test results and/or Michigan State Police labs
5. Dispatch logs
6. 911 and dispatch recordings
7. In-car dash cam videos
8. Booking/Datamaster video
9. Miranda warnings waiver sheet
10. Chemical test right sheet
11. Accident reports
12. Client and/or witness statements
13. Photographs
14. Personnel file of the officers
15. Datamaster calibration records/test results

16. Gas Chromatography Michigan State Police records

(36) DISCOVERY IN FELONY CASES

While the discovery process remains remarkably similar when it comes to a misdemeanor DUI vs a felony DUI, there are an especially important key consideration.

If a felony DUI is charged based on it being a third or more offense, it will be important to track down records of the prior cases along with the sentence imposed. If the prosecutor is using out-of-state convictions as the basis of the Michigan charge, there may be an opportunity to challenge these priors as a basis for the felony. It is important to understand what the prior sentences were because it will assist in crafting a potential outcome in the present case.

For example, if the client has prior DUI offenses, and in their prior sentences, they never received counseling, either outpatient or inpatient, it may help to make an argument that the client does not need jail, but rather should have the opportunity to receive treatment.

If the felony DUI is charged based on causation of a serious bodily injury or death, the discovery will be a lot more expansive, and include accident reconstruction, medical records, autopsy reports etc.

Felony cases also differ in that a preliminary examination is available to the defense to challenge the case, but sometimes more realistically to simply conduct further discovery during this process. A well-planned cross-examination of witnesses at the preliminary examination can be fruitful is learning more about the case, but also it may lead to the discovery of additional information, which may not have been apparent before putting a witness on the stand. A preliminary examination can be a test-drive of the prosecution's case without the risk of being found guilty of the charge. Typically, once the examination is complete, a new judge is assigned to the case, and a new prosecutor will take over.

A felony DUI carries severe driver's license ramifications and mandatory jail time, so the preliminary examination is a key component to both challenging and learning more about the strengths and weaknesses of the case. This information is invaluable when it comes to leveraging plea deals from a prosecutor, sentencing agreements from a judge, and preparing for trial.

(37) Being proactive

Getting the best deal from the prosecutor

When charged with a DUI offense in Michigan, a client has two options. The client can sit back, let their attorney do their job, and hope that things work out in the end. The other approach has the client equally engaged daily; this is the proactive approach, which all my clients must do from day one.

I am very selective in who I agree to take on as a client; I am looking for motivated clients who are looking to change the perception of their case daily. When a client is arrested and charged with a DUI, the perception of the police, prosecutor, judge and the community is my client is a dangerous person and cannot be trusted to make good choices with alcohol or driving. When a client's freedom and ability to drive can be taken away, it is time to get serious about changing this perception.

If I agree to take on a client, I provide the tools and resources for that client to be proactive on day one. Each case is different, and each program is customized, but generally the program involves an alcohol screening and assessment, alcohol education and/or treatment, attendance at AA meetings, proactive volunteer work, alcohol and drug testing among other components.

If my client follows my lead, it helps open options for our case. All DUI cases in Michigan are either resolved with litigation (motions, hearings or trial) or resolution (plea bargain with prosecutor).

As a former prosecutor in Michigan and New York City, I have worked out 1000's of deals on both ends of the table. All cities, township and county prosecutors have a different litmus tests for plea bargaining, and each case is different. Most DUI cases have some ugly elements to it; prior criminal history, prior DUI history, high BAC reading, accident, client is under 21, rude behavior by my client to the police, along with a handful of other potential issues.

When it comes to resolving these cases, I need to overcome many negative facts in my client's case, and my words alone can only go so far. All clients have jobs they cannot lose, all clients need to drive to work and to take care of their family, nobody can afford to go to jail, and nobody wants a DUI on their record.

These factors DO NOT make you unique when charged with a DUI. The more successful you are, the more professional licenses you hold, and the better career you have, the higher the standard is set by the prosecutor and judge. Just because you have been a doctor for 30 years, does not mean a thing to a prosecutor, if anything it will be held against you for knowing better than getting yourself in this situation.

While I present my client's past, present and where they are going in the future, this is not enough to distinguish my client. Because my client has spent weeks if not months being proactive, I can drop these accomplishments on the prosecutor and distinguish my client from the other names in the prosecutor's stack of files.

These proactive accomplishments can be the difference between having or not having a drunk driving conviction on your record, losing or keeping your license, going to jail, having an interlock on your car for a year, having your car immobilized more points on your license, higher fines, costs and driver responsibility fees and other major differences.

By following my proactive program, you are helping your case every single day, and putting yourself in the best position to reach the best resolution within the context of your case.

As the client makes progress on the program, I proudly share this information with the prosecutor in order to educate them on how you are different than their typical case. I have set a high bar with past clients, so prosecutors are almost expecting my clients to be rock stars.

Further, I lay out the client accomplishments in a memorandum to the prosecutor along with proposed motion that I would file if the case cannot be resolved. As a former prosecutor I provide this information in a very respectful way to the other side, and keep the door open for resolution, but I am firm in the possibility of litigating the case. This approach gives my client the best of both worlds.

(38) Being proactive

Getting the best sentence

from the judge

If my client has followed the proactive program, we have likely resolved the case with the prosecutor in a very favorable way. This may have meant a reduction in charges, down to a lower drunk driving charge, or to a non-drunk driving offense.

No matter what deal we work out with the prosecutor, the judge is aware of what the original charge was and could simply treat the sentence as if my client plead guilty to the original higher charge. An example of this would be if my client were originally charged with Operating with a High BAC and say their BAC level was 0.24. If I can leverage my client's proactive achievements into a reduction in charges to Operating While Intoxicated, or even better, the judge may still focus on the original facts of the case.

Although having the High BAC charge avoids a mandatory ignition interlock on your case, a judge can still make that part of your sentence even if you plead to a lower charge. Same can be said about things like mandatory jail time on second offenses if we are able to get the charge reduced to a first offense.

Same goes with probation. Most impaired drunk driving cases receive 6 to 12 months of probation, while a High BAC case tends to be 12 to 24 months. If your case is reduced from High BAC to Impaired Driving, you would think you would receive the typical Impaired sentence, but most judges will still treat it like the more serious charge. These situations are why my proactive program is so important.

When a client of mine resolves a case with an impressive reduction in charges, I make the point to explain to the judge WHY the reduction was made; my client earned it, it wasn't just handed over to get rid of the case. I want the judge to know that despite some of the unfavorable facts in the case, my client has already started the process of moving on and learn from the situation, which we hope and believe was, and will be isolated.

It is also my goal to cover many parts of a sentence in advance. For example, if I know a judge typically sentences a client to 50 hours of community service, I will have my client do it ahead of time. It's better for my client to pick the organization, spend their time with the organization without the "court ordered" cloud over their head, and not have the penalty of jail hanging over their head if they fail to accomplish the community service. I also do not want my clients being ordered to pick-up trash on the side of the road in the winter.

We do the same for AA meetings, alcohol education/treatment and having a substance abuse assessment done ahead of time. Ideally, our own professional is doing the evaluation, and not the one hand picked by the court.

We may also be able to do what is known as same day sentencing if we have done the evaluation ahead of time. This saves my client at least two trips to court, a meeting with probation, and starts the clock on probation. When you are ordered to return for sentencing, this could be two months later, which basically adds two months to your probation.

(39) BEING PROACTIVE DAMAGE CONTROL FOR THE PROBATION VIOLATION

When a client is put on probation, this means the judge decided that a jail sentence was not appropriate at the time of sentencing. This does not mean that jail is completely off the table, and it does not mean that your sentence is final.

While on probation, there are several conditions to follow, and plenty of requirements to complete. For this reason, I try to have my client complete their sentence proactively so there are little to no requirements remaining.

Some common conditions of probation are no new criminal offenses, no use of alcohol and/or drugs, no travel outside of Michigan without permission of the court and to make truthful reports to probation.

Some common sentencing requirements are payment of fines and costs, community service, attendance at AA, counseling, educational classes and regular alcohol and drug testing. Failure to adhere to these conditions and requirements means a show cause hearing with your judge and a petition by probation to violate you.

If you violate your probation, the judge has a few options. The judge cannot do anything, which is rare, the judge can extend your probation to a longer period, add additional community service, counseling and testing or send you to jail. Depending upon your criminal history, the present offense and the severity of the violation, all of these are possible.

If sent to jail, you are still going to be on probation when you come out.

When I work with a client who has been show caused or faces a probation violation, I put proactive actions into place immediately. Just like regular sentencing, we need to demonstrate a willingness to learn from the situation and get back on track. I anticipate what the probation department may recommend to the judge, and what the judge will do with my client.

All clients are entitled to contest the violation, but in my career as a prosecutor and defense lawyer, I have only seen a handful of successful attempts of going this route, because the proof standard is lower for violations.

Assuming that my client's goal is to "resolve" the violation with the judge, we must go above and beyond what a judge may be thinking and come up with jail alternatives.

For a DUI case in Michigan, a probation violation usually means being rearrested for a new DUI or missing or failing a scheduled alcohol or drug test. A brand-new DUI arrest is big trouble. Most judges are ready to throw my client in jail, especially if it happened within the court's jurisdiction. A failed or missed test is also serious, but a client is less likely to receive jail time in this scenario.

Depending upon the level of violation, my client will increase their testing proactively. I may have my client volunteer to wear an alcohol tether, test 2-3 times per day on a home-testing device, and my client might check themselves into intensive outpatient or inpatient counseling or attend an Impact Weekend. If we can self-impose tougher testing and setup a jail alternative than we have a much better shot at avoiding jail, and other devastating sanctions.

(40) BEING PROACTIVE

PROACTIVE STEPS TO A BETTER LIFE

Yes, being proactive is mandatory when you work with me, and yes, it is mostly geared to help us with the prosecutor, judge and probation, but in the end, it could save my client's life. Most clients come to me for a DUI after the worst night of their life, and something led to this moment in time. My client may be having trouble at work, medical issues, trouble at home or simply have an out of control substance abuse issue. A client comes to me for help inside the courtroom, but I probably help them even more outside of the courtroom.

I see clients at their worst; they come to me with everything on the line. A client's freedom is on the line, finances are about to get tight, and their ability to drive is in jeopardy. Sometimes my client is in a bad place medically, and without my help, will hurt themselves or someone else in the community.

I've yet to work with a client who did not tell me during the case, or at the end of the case that my proactive program really helped them get their life together. The average DUI case in Michigan lasts about 8 weeks, and longer if we go to trial. Many of my client's cases are not completed until 6-12 months after the actual DUI incident happened.

During a DUI case in Michigan, a court at most is doing some alcohol and drug testing, but the client can drive without restriction, and free to live their life however they wish. There is not much to stop a client from drinking and driving at this point in the case; if the client has an alcohol problem, the addiction will be stronger than fear of a bond violation. Sometimes a case takes a while to be charged, and a client can have weeks and months go by before a court is even monitoring them for drugs and alcohol.

This is exactly why I require all my clients to go on my proactive plan from day one. Even if the result is a dismissal of charges, or a not guilty at trial, the client still found themselves arrested and charged with a DUI offense. This is enough of a reason to make changes in your life and put several safety measures (for the client, their family and the community) in place.

Not only will the program help once we are in court, but I need a sober and clear-minded client to assist me during the case. I need a client who has sweat equity in the result, and a I need a client who is learning from the case no matter the outcome.

My ideal case result for a client is the following:

Client comes to me after a DUI arrest. Depending upon criminal history and the facts of the case, the client begins proactive alcohol testing to hold themselves accountable from day one. The client is not using illegal drugs, and they pass a 10-panel drug screen, and they test daily for alcohol. The client undergoes an alcohol screening and assessment and follows the recommendation (education and or/treatment) and attends AA on a weekly basis. I may also send the client to an Impact Weekend or intensive outpatient or inpatient counseling.

As my client is making changes in their life, and holding themselves accountable, I am working all angles on their behalf to have their case dismissed via motion or at a hearing and come up with potential trial defense. Best case, we make the case go away, but my client has learned from the situation, and will never put themselves in the same situation again. I also hope that their family and friends can learn from the situation, and the case has a broad impact on society in an incredibly positive way.

I have had clients share their stories with friends and family, which have inspired those people to be more aware of their own decisions. Outsiders see my client who is otherwise successful and put together and realize that no one is immune to getting in trouble while behind the wheel.

The worst thing would be for a client to get off, not learn from it, assume they will get off the next time, and continue this dangerous pattern of bad choices. Nobody likes drunk driving; every single one of my client's would agree as well, and it is my job that my clients learn, and avoid the same pitfalls in the future.

It would be a disservice to the community if I were enabling bad behavior; I drive on the same roads, as does my family and friends; I want to prevent future DUI's just as much as law enforcement.

(41) BEING PROACTIVE

SPECIAL CONSIDERATIONS FOR A DUI FELONY

I have already covered how my proactive program helps inside the courtroom with the prosecutor, judge, probation and outside the courtroom in my client's life, but I also wanted touch on a few additional thoughts on felony DUI cases.

When you are charged with a felony in Michigan, prison is now on the table. In Michigan, a jail sentence is a firm number, and usually ends up being less time served. When sentenced to prison, you only get a minimum number, but the maximum always remains in place; you must also be paroled out; there is no automatic return home date. Going to prison for a DUI case in Michigan can mean an exceptionally long time away from your friends and family. Although a third DUI in Michigan could mean up to 5 years in prison, and a DUI causing death could be 15 years in prison, jail is still the most likely outcome for felony cases.

In fact, for a DUI third offense, there is a mandatory 30-day jail sentence that must be imposed by the judge. While work-release, house arrest and other alternatives were used in the past by judges, most Michigan judges are now following the 30-day jail minimum without these alternatives. In fact, most judges I come across usually have 60 to 120 days jail in mind when it comes to a third offense DUI.

When I work with a client who is charged with a third offense DUI, we may be able to work toward a misdemeanor reduction, which avoids a felony record, 5 years' worth of prison on the table, possibility of keeping a driver's license, and the mandatory jail sentence. This is quite rarely offered, but in some Michigan counties it is a real possibility. This result does not just happen, it must be earned, and my program provides the tools and resources to get it done, and get it done well.

The first thing any client who is charged with a felony DUI does on my program is begin testing 2-3 times per day daily for alcohol. There is zero benefit of the doubt from anyone once you have had 3 or more DUI arrests. The client will also get into intensive counseling and hit an AA meeting 3-5 times per week. These are minimal considerations. I typically add a few other requirements into the mix.

Getting my client started on the program provides the client an opportunity to climb out of the very deep hole they have dug for themselves. It is likely their own families and friends have turned on them at this point, and the community views them as nothing more than an extremely dangerous and untrustworthy criminal. I try to provide the client with something new, something they have never had in their life.

I offer a rigorous program, providing structure and unlimited opportunity to change the perception of their case. Following my lead could mean avoiding a felony, jail, prison and loss of the ability to drive. Each felony DUI in Michigan presents its own challenges, but also opportunities to create a healthier client and a safer community. I will not even consider a client charged with a felony DUI if they are not willing to dig in deep and follow my lead 100 percent.

(42) CHALLENGING A PRIOR DUI CONVICTION

When I represent a DUI client with prior DUI offenses, it is important to discuss the year of the offense, the court and the circumstances behind the case. Most of the time, a prior DUI offense is permanent, and can escalate the present-day case into a second or third offense. It could also cause the Secretary of State to take more severe sanctions on your driver's license.

For the prosecutor to prevail on either a plea or a guilty verdict for a second or third offense, they must prove the Defendant has prior convictions. Most of the time, the prior convictions are stipulated by the parties, but there are exceptions.

Occasionally a client provides me information about a prior case, and there might be an opportunity to potentially a prior DUI conviction, and which would assist the present-day case.

An example of how to challenge a prior offense would be if the client plead guilty in the past, but was without legal counsel, hence the plea could be invalid. It would require going back to the original court to make this challenge; it does not mean the old case goes away, but it would take away the "prior" for the new case.

This technique would require obtaining the old transcripts and court documents to invalidate the past plea.

(43-44) Driver's License Considerations

When charged with a DUI in Michigan, there are several consequences; one of those consequences is impact on your driver's license. The court has no say over what happens to your license, because the Michigan Secretary of State is the lone authority on what happens to your ability to drive if convicted of DUI offense.

The Michigan Secretary of State can only sanction a Michigan driver's license, which means if you have an out of state license, Michigan cannot do anything other than control your ability to drive within the State, but not outside of the State.

The Secretary of State can either restrict, suspend or revoke a driver's license. A restriction allows some driving, typically to school, work, medical appointments, community service, counseling, court and a few other exceptions. A suspension can take away the driver's ability to drive for a limited period, and once the time passes, the driving privileges resume. Revocation is a lifetime loss of driving privileges, but they can be restored by the Secretary of State at a future, but uncertain date.

License impact depends upon the type of conviction. Here is a brief breakdown of the most common offenses.

- Impaired Driving - 90 days restricted driving

- Zero Tolerance - 30 days restricted driving
- Intoxicated Driving/Drugged Driving - 30-day suspension, 150 days restricted
- Super Drunk - 45 days restricted driving, 320 restricted with ignition interlock installed
- Second Offense - 1-year suspension
- Third Offense - license revoked, eligible to reapply after 1 year

In Michigan, the criminal penal code says it is a second offense if you have two convictions within seven years; the date of offense is used on the subsequent offense to make this determination. So, if you were convicted on September 2nd, 2001, you would fall into the second offense category if you are subsequently arrested on or before September 2nd, 2008. For a third or more offense, there is no time limit; it is simply within a lifetime. So, you can have a conviction from 1950, 1999 and 2016.

There is not much strategy in timing when it comes to the criminal code; the best approaches are defeating the case, or resolution with a reduction, sobriety court or sentencing agreement. While timing for the criminal code cannot be impacted, it is the exact opposite when it comes to the Secretary of State.

The Secretary of State has the same seven-year mark for second offenses, but they use the conviction date for measuring this period.

This means that if you were convicted of a DUI on September 2nd of 2001, and subsequently arrested in the summer of 2008, there is a lot of strategy involved. If my client has decided to resolve the case or even go to trial, we make sure the "end" of the case takes place after September 2nd of that year, which would put us outside of the seven-year window. The client if convicted would be treated as a first offender outside of the seven-year window.

This strategy could mean the difference between losing his/her ability to drive for a full year vs being restricted for 90 days. This same strategy is even more crucial when it comes to third offenses.

Unlike the criminal penal code, the Secretary of State does use a ten-year window. Many of my clients have two incredibly old DUI's from 10 to 20 years ago. While they will still be charged as a third offender, they can escape the license sanctions for a third offender with the right timing. There is a chance a third offender could be treated as a second offender, or even a first offender with the right timing strategy.

(45) & (46) FELONY CONSIDERATIONS BEAT THE CASE AT PRELIMINARY EXAMINATION & KEEP THE CASE AT THE DISTRICT COURT

If charged with a felony DUI in Michigan, your case will begin at the district court level with a preliminary examination. This would be a third offense or more, or a case, which caused serious bodily injury or death.

If charged with a felony, you are entitled to this hearing within 21 days of your arraignment, but can waive this timeframe if you wish to invest more time in conducting discovery, or working a proactive plan in order to open up some options for resolution.

A preliminary examination is put in place to "test" the evidence before the case can go to the circuit court level. The "test" is probable cause; is it probable based on the evidence that a crime was committed, which is named in the information, and is this the person that probably committed it. This is not a test of guilt or innocence, but a safeguard put in place to make sure that someone is not charged based on very thin or problematic evidence.

If there is enough evidence your case is "bound over" to the circuit court. This can be done by holding the examination and having the judge weigh the evidence, or both sides can agree to a waiver.

Many innocent people are "bound" over, because in DUI cases, there is usually enough evidence that it is probable the person arrested broke the law in some way with alcohol or a controlled substance.

For example, there may be evidence that the Defendant tested over the legal limited or had marijuana in their system when driving. That would make it probable that a crime was committed, but not quite guilty. This book is filled with defenses to cases where the Defendant "looks guilty".

So how do you beat the case at preliminary exam? You can beat the case in two ways. An outright dismissal of charges, or a reduction down to a misdemeanor.

First, outright dismissal is rare for a DUI case, because there will usually be some triable facts, which are better resolved at trial, but what if there is concrete evidence that the Defendant was not the driver? What if it turns out that the roadway, which the Defendant operated was not open or accessible to the public? What if the traffic stop was bogus and the officer lacked a legal reason for conducting a traffic stop? These, and many other situations could lead to a dismissal.

Second, a limited number of counties in Michigan will consider dismissing a felony DUI case and reducing in down to a misdemeanor. This is a possibility if the current charge is a "true third" meaning you have only had two prior offenses.

It helps if the priors are deeper in the past, and not recent, and if the BAC number is somewhat on the lower end of the spectrum, and there was no accident.

I've been able to have a lot of felony DUI cases dropped to misdemeanors, but those particular cases had clients who worked their butt off on my proactive program, and were willing to make major commitments to sobriety including daily testing, intensive treatment, and sometimes sobriety court or jail alternative programs like Impact Weekend.

If the case is reduced to a misdemeanor then it will be handled at the district court level, because a felony is now off the timetable along with prison time. A judge will still consider your past offenses but has less in his/her bag of sentencing tricks because the offense is now a misdemeanor. The prosecutor decides the charge, the judge decides the sentence.

(47) Drug offenses – Marijuana Zero Tolerance standard

If I polled 100 people in Michigan who smoke marijuana, I bet half of those people would not know that driving a car in Michigan is illegal with any amount of marijuana in their system. Many of them assume that they must be somehow "under the influence" of the drug, which impacts their ability to drive. Without a medical marijuana card in Michigan, the standard is "presence" meaning zero tolerance.

Many scientific studies have concluded that there is no link between THC levels and your ability to drive. In fact, many states acknowledge that, and have not adopted the zero-tolerance standard like Michigan. In Michigan, any amount of active THC in your system will trigger a crime if you drive a car. It can be as little as 1 nanogram.

Recent Michigan case law has held that inactive THC such as COOH-THC also known as 11-Nor-9-Carboxy-THC, which is the secondary metabolite of THC is NOT against the law to have it in your system while driving. While the law is still out of sync with the data on impairment, this ruling brought Michigan law closer to reality.

This means that you would have had to smoke marijuana within a few hours of driving to trigger a crime, because anything beyond a few hours should only leave the inactive metabolites. Without this ruling, one could technically smoke marijuana on May 1st, quit for 29 days and drive a car on May 30th, and still have inactive THC in their blood.

(48) Drug offenses - Marijuana

Presence not enough for cardholders

While Michigan has adopted a general zero tolerance "presence" test for marijuana, this DOES NOT apply to medical marijuana cardholder under the Michigan Marijuana Act (MMMA). The *Koon* decision held that the MMMA trumps the Motor Vehicle Code's provision which outlaws the operation of a car with active THC in one's system.

The standard under Michigan law for a cardholder is "under the influence" like a drunk driving case involving alcohol. The only difference is there is no legal limit like the 0.08 BAC level for alcohol. For marijuana, the test of this standard is a bit vaguer. The burden of showing "under the influence" is of course on the prosecutor.

A prosecutor will look to introduce the Defendant's performance on field sobriety tests and the Drug Evaluation and Classification Program, which consists of 12 steps that evaluate the Defendant. The prosecutor may also rely on an expert witness to convey what if anything the levels indicate from the blood draw, and how the marijuana could put a driver under the influence. It is certainly more difficult for a prosecutor to proof "under the influence" for marijuana than alcohol.

(49) Blood Results

Challenge the Search Warrant

If you are arrested for a DUI in Michigan, a police officer gets to select which of the three chemical tests you need to take to comply with the Implied Consent law. If you refuse the officer, he/she can obtain a warrant for a blood draw at a local medical facility. This then triggers the Implied Consent license sanctions, which I discuss in another section of this book. For now, let us just look at how one can challenge a search warrant, which lead to a blood draw result. If successful, the result itself would not be admissible against you.

In Michigan, the standard to obtain a search warrant for a blood draw is probable cause that the person to be tested committed a DUI offense as outlined in the Motor Vehicle Code. Essentially an officer needs to piece together his observations, tests conducted and the circumstances to ask a judge or magistrate to sign an order to compel a blood draw. Without the probable cause, a warrant will not be issued, and if it is, and it is challenged, the results would not be admissible.

One piece of evidence commonly relied upon by the police to obtain a search warrant is a PBT result. Although not admissible at trial, it is admissible for purposes of justifying an arrest and seeking a warrant for a blood draw. Other factors would be statements by the Defendant about consumption of alcohol or drugs, observations by the police, and performance on field sobriety tests. Obtaining the video and audio from the incident is helpful in "challenging" these elements, which lead to the issuance of the warrant. If we can show that the puzzle, which was pieced together to get the search warrant does not quite fit together than we stand a good chance of challenging the warrant.

It then becomes a situation where we all know the BAC level was potentially over the limit, but because of a technicality, it may not be admissible against you. This does not mean your case is dismissed based on this, but the prosecutor would need to go forward without their most powerful piece of evidence, and may look to make a deal, or could get beat at a trial.

(50) Blood Results - Get an Independent Test

In Michigan, the police will undoubtedly obtain a chemical test result from you either by breath, blood or urine. While that is usually the only test conducted in a DUI case, it does not mean it is the only one allowed.

In Michigan, a Defendant has the right to obtain their own independent blood test after the police have conducted one of the three tests. Many do not even know this is a possibility, and for the most part the result will probably not vary, but if you have concerns about the integrity of the test, then you should consider this option. As you're reading this book, it's of course too late to go out and get a blood test, so this section of the book will focus on what happens if you DID request one, but you were not allowed to have it performed.

If you requested an independent, and it was "reasonable", the original test result won't be suppressed, but it would be possible to get a jury instruction stating that the police violated the Defendant's right to this test, and they can therefore assign whatever weight they want to this circumstance. It may be favorable to discredit the one chemical test by theorizing that a second test was an option, but the police denied this "double-check" opportunity. It is certainly a way to get creative with one's arguments.

Of course, the one downside of requesting an independent exam is the result coming back close to the original, or potentially higher.

In this situation, you would have the mandated test come back at 0.17, and now you request your own, and it comes back at 0.17 or 0.19. Any good prosecutor can now argue that the first test was accurate, and given a chance to confirm the result, it came back accurate on the second - this was a test that the Defendant asked for, and you have the same or higher result; most if not all doors of discrediting the tests are closed by a confirming test.

(51) Blood Results Whole blood vs serum blood

When arrested for a DUI in Michigan, the police can pick from three different chemical tests, blood, urine or breath. A blood test can vary depending upon the purpose of the initial blood draw. When the blood is drawn, it could either be calculated as whole or serum blood. This is dangerous proposition for a client because serum blood will come back at a higher BAC than whole blood. A conversion must be done in order to get an accurate result. The law requires that serum blood be converted to a whole blood equivalent.

The blood is usually serum when drawn for medical purposes, which is analyzed at the hospital rather than a criminal case, which is analyzed at a forensic laboratory; the blood will be serum if the blood is drawn to begin for purposes of a criminal case. A hospital uses an enzymatic method that tests blood serum; whole blood in comparison contains cellular material and proteins that clot.

The difference in process comes down to hospitals will centrifugate whole blood, which means spinning it, which eliminates solids and leaves only a serum, which is a higher concentration, which results in a higher BAC level. Serum blood can contain 1.6 more alcohol than whole blood, which could turn a 0.07 to a 0.11, which is a major difference when working on a DUI case in Michigan.

Any blood result attributed to my client in a Michigan DUI case is first examined to make sure we are working with the whole blood number, and not an elevated serum number. Sometimes this requires contacting the hospital to obtain the documentation that occupied the blood result.

I run into these sort of issues in accident cases where my client is rushed to the hospital for medical purposes, examined, treated and cared for, but not investigated and charged until the "medical" portion of the case is over. The hospital draws blood as part of their process, but not to prosecute, but rather to treat. Sometimes we need to convert this in order to protect my client from being prosecuted with an unfairly elevated number.

(52) Challenging Blood Test Results Gas Chromatography 101

In Michigan, blood samples are tested by the Michigan State Police; the MSP use the flame ionization gas chromatograph blood analysis process. This process is reliable, but it has sources of error, uncertainty, and must be performed in a scientifically acceptable way.

The prosecutor is required by the constitution to produce the witness who conducted the analysis of the blood sample. This blood sample is not the entire sample, but rather a small portion of it. This small amount of blood is combined with t-butanol and n-propanol. The mixture is heated, and a needle draws what is known as the "headspace" from the vial.

Headspace is the gas space above the sample in a chromatography vial. Volatile sample components diffuse into the gas phase, forming the headspace gas. Headspace analysis is therefore the analysis of the components present in that gas.

The headspace is then blown into a gas chromatograph by carrier gas, which for the MSP is helium. The vial is capped with a buta rubber stopper that the needle punctures to draw the headspace gas from the mixture. There are studies available that say not to use this rubber stopper, because it could absorb the organic compounds in the vial, which would alter the mix, which would compromise the sample. If this rubber stopper absorbs the t-butanol or the n-propanol, then the alcohol concentration will be higher in the sample.

Along with the questionable use of the buta rubber stopper, the integrity of the concentration of the blood sample depends on the integrity of the vacuum seal of the initial blood collection from my client. Chemical solvents are used to maintain the blood from the point of the blood draw to the time when it enters the gas chromatograph process at the MSP lab. If this seal fails, then the sample is contaminated.

The administrative rules used by the MSP lab are less stringent than the accepted scientific principles. One alarming lack of stringency is the use of one controlled sample throughout the entire day instead of before and after each sample. This means that the machine is only tested when the doors open; if the machine is malfunctioning or not producing accurate results by lunch time, you're going to have a full afternoon of questionable results, which should not be used as evidence in a criminal case.

The MSP lab also does not follow the MIST 8-step protocol for use of an uncertainty budget aka sources of error. MSP's explanation for not following the strictest protocols is practicality, which is not acceptable to me.

(53) Challenging Blood Test Results Collection, transport & storage

The testing process in Michigan is only as good as the integrity of the sample, and there are a lot of issues with how these samples are collected, transported and stored.

The process works this way: the blood is drawn from the client; the blood is sealed in the Tri-Tech kit. The officer then mails the sample to the MSP lab. Once the sample is received, it is stored in a temperature-controlled unit.

So, the sample is not temperature controlled for multiple days as it is tossed around as it travels from step to step. This is like leaving raw chicken out for 5 days, sticking it in the fridge for an hour then cooking it, and serving it to your kids.

The so-called additives added to the sample to preserve the sample are delayed as it awaits the refrigeration process, which allows for metabolization of the glucose at 5-7 percent an hour if kept at room temperature. When was the last time a mail truck was room temperature in the hot summer or a below zero winter? Without the right controlled temperature, the fermentation process will begin, and the sample is contaminated.

Other than the absurd lack of temperature control, the vacuum seal must be 100 percent sealed; any fault in that seal and the sample is further in question.

(54) Challenging Chemical Test Results Not Read your rights

In Michigan, a person arrested for a DUI offense must be read their statutory chemical test rights by the police officer. The rights are listed under MCL 257.625a(6)(b) and the chemical test can either be blood, breath or urine. This test will determine the presence and the amount of alcohol, controlled substance or both.

Because the results of a chemical test are admissible in court, these rights must be adhered to and administered properly. If not, the implied consent law does not kick in, and the test results may not be admissible against the Defendant.

Because most officers will simply read word for word from the chemical test form paperwork, it is rare to find a case where the rights were not read. It is important to review the audio or video from the case, which can help sort out the status of the rights, and if they were read correctly. If there were not read, or not complete in their reading, a motion to suppress the chemical test results would be warranted, and likely granted.

(55) CHALLENGING CHEMICAL TEST RESULTS NOT A CERTIFIED OPERATOR

When arrested for a DUI offense, the arresting officer may also be the officer who operates the Datamaster chemical test. This is usually a smooth transition and simplifies the prosecutor's case for a jury or judge. It does become an issue with the officer's license to operate the machine is non-existent.

The first thing we do is check the operator's card to see what class operator they are; this can range from class II, IIIA, IIB, IVA or IVB.

The weekly test is usually performed locally by a resident Datamaster operator, while the 120-day calibrations must be done by a Class IV operator.

If for some reason the operator is not qualified, then the results are sure to be suppressed due to lack of following the administrative rules. This may or may not require a motion before the court, or a prosecutor will apply common sense, verify the lack of qualifications and move to dismiss the case.

In the alternative the prosecutor may decide to go forward without the test results, but that would be an uphill battle to rely simply on officer observations and questionable field sobriety tests.

(56) Challenging Chemical Test Results

No 15 Minutes observed

In Michigan, if a Datamaster chemical test is offered by the police, current Michigan law states that before administering the Datamaster, there must be a 15-minute waiting period of observation. The observation time is to ensure that the person does not smoke, throw up or put anything in their mouth. If any of these three occur then the result of the test could, and likely is tainted. Because cops and prosecutors do not like to have evidence suppressed this rule was created, but not always followed.

When I first take on a case, one of the first things that I look at is the evidence ticket from the Datamaster. I look for the start observation time and the time of the first sample provided. If there is not 15-minutes built in, then the results are ripe for suppression.

Along with the 15-minutes themselves, there also must be "observation" of my client. Recent case law has expanded what observation means; current cases say that the observer can look away for a moment, and the observation can be shared by multiple officers.

Although the interpretation of the rules has expanded, I see many cases where the officers still lack compliance and we are able to challenge the results. The only way I get my clients to the point of challenging the observation period is by using the information gathering stage (officially known as discovery).

The most helpful piece of information is the booking video, which should capture my client, where he/she is sitting, who if anyone is around them, and what they are doing during this time; most importantly making sure that the times line up correctly.

I have had a clock on the wall, the time on the video and the time on the evidence ticket all vary for observation and the test itself. Now this could have many explanations, but the one I go with, is that something is not right, and my client should not be prosecuted based on such questionable evidence, and we move for suppression.

(57) CHALLENGING CHEMICAL TEST RESULTS RADIO INTERFERENCE

In Michigan, police officers use the Datamaster machine to test breath samples; this device is electronic and subject to the same interference as other devices that generate electrical power. One kind of interference that is possible is radio frequency interference or RFI.

Although the machine apparently has a built-in sensor, which is designed to seek and identify this sort of interference, there is no guideline or information about how sensitive the sensor is during the tests. Just like a metal detector; some may pick up the metal on your belt, and some may not, but we all know there is metal being undetected. The same holds true for radio interference; we know there are radios in and around a police station, potentially even right next to the device if the officer has one; if the sensor doesn't go off, does that actually mean something? It has my position that there is always the possibility of some radio interference, even if the sensor does not pick it up.

In my experience there are at least five types of radio interference that must be detected, many which may not be picked up with a low sensitivity sensor.

It is imperative to test for radio interference from mobile transmitters from patrol cars, ambulances and fire trucks, even news trucks driving around and private citizens using them. It must test for military and private security radio, base radio communication from the police station itself, portable transmitters from handheld police radios and a scenario where all of them are acting in concert.

It's not a stretch to have a situation where the police station is surrounded by private citizens transmitting radio signals, military operations being conducted in the airspace, each cop having his own radio on his person, multiple police cars, and emergency vehicles transmitting and the police station itself (where the test is being conducted) sending out various signals to those same cars and officers.

Many prosecutors, police officers and judges roll their eyes at radio interference, and I really don't quite understand why? It is likely that the attorney presenting it moved on too quick without having the witness acknowledge all the possibilities, and the fact that we have no idea how sensitive the device is or is not.

Another problem area, which goes unchallenged is the machine only conducts a test at the very beginning; some of these tests take 10 to 15 minutes. Radio waves come and go, especially at a busy police station, and to simply ignore further tests is absurd. Some states have acknowledged this gap by placing shields on the device, but Michigan has not done so, which is an excellent issue to put in front of a jury to challenge the test results. In my view, until a shield is adopted by

Michigan then no Datamaster test is actually fully reliable; how can a jury believe beyond a reasonable doubt that the test was accurate when a neighboring state doubted their same tests, and added the extra precaution.

(58) Challenging Chemical Test Results

Not maintained/tested properly

In Michigan, the Datamaster machine must be maintained and tested properly for it to work properly. The machine determines the fate of tens of thousands of people in Michigan each year, and the machine cannot be treated like your car.

Sticking with the car analogy, law enforcement must always rotate their tires, get scheduled oil changes and always be operating within the most stringent guidelines; essentially getting the maximum gas mileage and performance always. If there is a lapse in these guidelines, then the test is not reliable and should be suppressed.

In Michigan, the rules say a class II, IIIA, IIIB or IVB operator must verify every machine on weekly basis using a vapor solution provided by Michigan State Police or using a compressed alcohol gas device that delivers exactly .080 grams of alcohol per 210 liters of vapor. Based on this deliverance, the machine MUST record a result of .076 to .084. Recent case law has ruled that the weekly compliance rule will not automatically suppress the result, but rather it will factor into the weight of the evidence for a judge or jury to determine.

When I get a case, I order the Datamaster logs, and see how the machine was testing before and after my client's test was performed. Courts have ruled that attack of the logs is permissible and the other test results are admissible as a factor for a judge or jury to consider.

Along with the weekly test, the Datamaster needs to be inspected and verified for accuracy and cleanliness every 120 days by a class IVB operator or a representative from the manufacturer.

If the rules were not followed, or the machine is providing a number outside of the range then it should be attacked. You have two swings at this issue; pre-trial motion requesting that the judge suppress the results, and/or at trial where you can challenge the weight of the results, but they'd be admitted for a judge or jury to hear.

These techniques may require an expert to educate a judge or jury on what weight if any should be attributed to the results. In addition to the overall weight, it may be possible to use the results to one's advantage.

If I am working on a case where my client recorded a 0.08 or even 0.09 on the Datamaster, and after looking at the logs, the machine is "testing high" at 0.084, we know the machine is turning the 0.08 into a higher number, which helps me argue that it's possible, if not likely that my client actually could have blown a 0.076, but was only elevated by the margin of error allowed by the machine.

Finally, another method I like to point out to a jury is the machine being tested with a 0.08 solution. That's probably a good idea for a case where my client blew a 0.08, as the jury knows that number could actually be 0.076 or 0.084, but if my client allegedly blew a 0.18, the machine was not tested for accuracy for what my client actually blew. This is like hitting the popcorn button on your microwave for everything. Would you hit the popcorn button to reheat iced cold chicken? No, and that is how we attack the test result.

(59) Challenging Chemical Test Results

Reasonable Period of time

In drunk driving cases, there will always be a time where a cop or witness observe the Defendant driving a car. This moment in time establishes when someone was driving, which can then be evaluated with the time that the chemical test was performed.

Recent case law eliminated the "reasonable period of time" rule in Michigan, and said the above scenario is enough to determine how much weight to give the result rather than to have it suppressed via pretrial motion by a judge. If 60 minutes pass between the first point of observed operation or 3 hours, that is for a jury to decide, and not a judge, which has led to more trials.

There is a remaining exception to the elimination of the reasonable period, which is the single-car accident because the operation time cannot be determined, because there is no eyewitness to the driving. If someone hits a deer, and there is nobody around to determine the time, then we have no idea when the driver last operated. Unless the Defendant provides this information then there is no way to know, and courts have said under this scenario it is possible for a judge to determine that such an extensive or unknown time delay could make the test result irrelevant, and suppressible before getting in front of a jury at trial. If my client was involved in a single-car accident, and the last moment of operation cannot be determined then we may move for suppression of the results due to a lack of reasonable time period.

This technique puts the burden on the prosecutor to show the test is relevant by establishing operation. If they cannot do that then the tests are simply not reliable; my client could have been passed out in his car for three hours before someone else gets eyes on my client.

(60) Challenging Chemical Test Results

Medical Conditions

If a Datamaster was used in your case, the police and prosecutor are no doubt convinced that it is 100 percent accurate. After all, their machine told them so, and machines never make errors. This machine not only NEVER makes errors in their mind, it also is completely reliable no matter who the test subject is; this stance is wrong and should be challenged. If the results are successfully challenged, a prosecutor is likely to dismiss their case, and you walk.

Each person who puts their mouth on the breath sample tube comes to it with different circumstances; a major one is preexisting medical conditions. There is a number of these medical conditions, which can make the test result completely unreliable.

If my client suffers from diabetes, and they are in a state of ketoacidosis, the elevated levels acetone in their blood could be wrongly identified as ethanol; the Datamaster machine does not know the difference. The same can be said for someone suffering from hypoglycemia.

If my client suffered a mouth or head injury as part of the case (car accident of some sort), it's very possible that they have blood in their mouth; even a small amount, which would not be detected by the police, could produce a "mouth alcohol" result, which is a higher concentration level, and the machine would be fooled into thinking a 0.02 is actually a 0.20.

The same can be said about recent or persistent regurgitation (throwing up/spitting up etc). This occurrence would cause alcohol from the stomach to be in your mouth, which if blown into the Datamaster would provide a much higher reading. It is a falsity to believe that the 15-minute observation rule or the machine itself would be able to make this distinction.

Another common issue that could impact the reliability of the results is Gastro Esophageal Reflux Disorder (GERD), which is a condition where alcohol is expelled from the stomach and enters the mouth, which would cause a false result.

Finally, if a client has dentures or any other dental issue, alcohol can get trapped in the mouth, which would create a higher concentration due to mouth alcohol.

(61) Challenging Chemical Test Results

Body temperature

Every person comes to the Datamaster machine with different characteristics; there are 100's of differences between me and you, and one of these is our body temperature. Not everyone has the same "normal" temperature, and people may be suffering from higher or lower levels due to both internal and external factors. Essentially, the higher your body temperature, the higher the breath alcohol result. I've yet to come across a case where the police officer takes my client's temperature. This is a problem for the test result.

The machine assumes that each person stepping up to the machine has a 98.6 Fahrenheit reading. Consider that scientific studies have said that one degree in variance, could cause a 7 percent variance in the test result. What if my client has the flu, and has a 100.6 temperature? That could artificially increase the result by 21 percent and could be the difference of winning or losing a trial.

(62) CHALLENGING CHEMICAL TEST RESULTS SUBSTANCES AFFECTING RESULT

The Datamaster can be impacted by many factors, and another one of these would be various substances in the test-takers body. Ethyl grain alcohol is what is against the law, and what the Datamaster is looking for, but it's very possible that substances such as ethyl ether, isopropyl alcohol, methyl alcohol, paraldehyde, acetone or trichloroethylene could lead to a misleading result.

Datamaster operators are not professionally trained or knowledgeable to detect or factor in the presence of stimulants, depressants, tranquilizers or hallucinogens, all of which could impact the test result. In DUI cases in Michigan, perception is everything. Even if a client did not use any of these, it does not matter. If the Datamaster operator acknowledges that these could impact the result, and they do not know of their status for my client, then this uncertainty should be enough to discredit the Datamaster result. The standard of proof is beyond a reasonable doubt, and that lack of certainty is a good reason to doubt and acquit.

(63) CHALLENGING CHEMICAL TEST RESULTS INFRARED SPECTROSCOPY 101

In Michigan, police agencies now use the Datamaster DMT for breath testing, which has replaced the BAC Datamaster. The new Datamaster uses infrared spectroscopy, which captures a sample of breath from the client. This sample may contain alcohol, which absorb infrared energy.

A known sample of infrared light is sent through the chamber, and if any ethanol is present, it absorbs that infrared light. The remaining light is measured by a detector; this "loss" of energy is then measured, and you get an alcohol reading. This measurement is only as accurate as the device and the procedure allows.

Before reaching this point, the machine goes through several steps including purging where the internal plumbing is cleansed of any residual substances from prior samples. If it is clear, there will be a .00 reading displayed. The machine will then do its ambient zeroing, which an interference filter is inserted in the infrared path to check for contaminants in the ambient air sample. These filters are used to separate ethanol from potential interference such as acetone.

The machine then does a blank test and a .000 will appear on the display if no contaminants are detected. The final step is the internal standard check where a quartz filter is dropped into the infrared light source path. The filter absorbs infrared energy, which is a known amount, determined during the calibration of the machine.

The infrared detector receives a reduced amount of infrared energy that was transmitted by the infrared source. The reduced intensity is evaluated by the microprocessor in the Datamaster, and a predetermined result is achieved. This step evaluates the machine's electronic system, signal analysis, and proceeding system to determine that everything is working properly.

While all these precautions sound impressive, they mean nothing if the machine does not alert the operator that some of these components that do the internal checks are not working properly.

Datamaster operators will testify under oath that there is a hole in the assumption that things are working properly, because they are not trained on anything other than pressing buttons, and rely on the machine itself to tell them that is working properly. This is like going to the doctor for a medical opinion, then coming back two minutes later for a second opinion, there is no true checks and balance system, because the machine checks itself.

(63) EXPUNGING A DUI CONVICTION

<u> This law change is currently on hold</u>**

If you or someone you love has been convicted of drunk driving in Michigan, there are now options available to have the conviction removed from your record. Prior to the law changing, someone convicted of drunk driving had to live the rest of their life with a criminal record. Under current Michigan law, we can now expunge a first offense drunk driving.

If someone has more than one drunk driving, there are other methods to be considered, and I would encourage you to read the next chaper, but for now, we are going to focus on first offense DUI's for expungement consideration.

Here is how the process works:
When someone files an expungement in Michigan, there are a lot of different agencies involved, and everyone needs to agree to expunge the DUI conviction.

1. Michigan State Police - they are the custodian of the Michigan DUI conviction and must verify your record.

2. Michigan Attorney General is asked to submit a response to the expungement request, and they can fight and advocate for your DUI

not to be expunged.

3. The original prosecutor on the case. Either the county, city, township, or village; whoever was the original prosecutor on your Michigan DUI will have an opportunity to object to your request and will appear in court to share their response with the judge.

4. The original judge makes the ultimate decision based upon the input of the other people involved in your case.

We will submit a comprehensive expungement application and supporting documents; above and beyond a few sheets of paper, which will likely be rejected by prosecutor and judge. This is a big request, removing a DUI from a criminal record has NEVER been done in Michigan under the expungement process. We need to take our very best shot. You have lived all these years with a drunk driving on your record, let's do this right!

When the new law was passed, the Prosecuting Attorneys Association of Michigan, the Michigan Sheriffs' Association and the Michigan Association of Chiefs of Police opposed the bill. Here is what they said when the new law was passed

"Prosecutors are concerned about the underlying dynamics of drunk driving and therefore couldn't philosophically support the policy," Matt

Wiese, president of the prosecutors association, said in a statement.

I anticipate that it will be an uphill battle to have DUI's expunged in Michigan, which is why I have created a dynamic approach to helping my clients give themselves the very best chance to erase the DUI from their record. Like my clients who come to me for new DUI's, my expungement DUI clients will be very proactive, organized, and comprehensive in their approach.

I look forward to discussing your DUI expungement with you. When you reach out, please have the following information available. Do not worry about formal records, we can help you track those down, but do your best to know the following:

1. The original court and judge
2. The year (exact date best) of when you were sentenced and were off probation. Again, I can help you with exact dates, but any information there will be helpful

I will likely have you walk me through what you have been doing since discharged from probation, such as career, education, family and community. We will help you get organized and put your best foot forward but be prepared to be an active participate in the process.

(63) APPLYING FOR A DUI PARDON

If you or someone you love has been convicted of drunk driving in Michigan, and it is not their first offense, they would not be eligible for expungement under the current law in Michigan. Although one door is closed, they are still eligible for a pardon. This applies no matter how many convictions they have, but the level of difficulty does rise for every additional conviction on their record.

I anticipate that under the new expungement law, a lot of people with two or three DUI's will reach out to me. Although more challenging, if your DUI cases are more than ten years old, or there is a significant reason or a major change in your life since your offenses, it would be worth exploring. I helped clients apply for pardons for first offenses under the old law, and I will continue to help clients with multiple convictions for drunk driving under the new law, but we would use the pardon process.

In Michigan, the Governor has what is called an executive clemency, which is listed in the Michigan Constitution. This power provides that the governor shall have power to grant reprieves, commutations, and pardons after convictions for all offenses, except cases of impeachment, upon such conditions and limitations as he may direct, subject to procedures and regulations prescribed by law.

The Michigan Supreme Court has held that the effect of a pardon by the Governor is such that it "releases the punishment and blots out of existence the guilt, so that in the eye of the law the offender is as innocent as if he had never committed the offense." People v. Van Heck, 252 Mich.App. 207, 216; 651 N.W.2d 174, 179 (2002).

While this outcome sounds like a dream come true, it is not the expectation, but rather the exception to the rule. When I agree to help a client with a pardon for multiple DUI offenses, we must go into it knowing that it is more likely than not, that the request will be denied, because that is what history tells us. Some requests are simply stronger cases than others. Most people believe that pardons are only for the well-connected, but I believe the pardon process was created for people who can demonstrate merit and have earned a second chance. Those are the people I help with the Michigan DUI pardon process.

A potential clemency application in my view must be supported at a minimum by documented sobriety since the conviction, a recent substance abuse evaluation from a licensed professional, documentation of education or employment since the incident, multiple letters of recommendation and a clear plan going forward.

I also find it helpful for a client to make both a written and video statement in support of their application. These statements should speak to why an exception should be made for their request to have a

DUI conviction removed from their record.

All applications for clemency begin with the Parole Board for review. The board will conduct a review of the merits. If the board does not find merit, it goes directly to the Governor with a denial recommendation. If the board does find merit, the request will then proceed to the next step.

Should the Governor grant a pardon request, the Governor's Office will issue the appropriate pardon documents, file the pardon with the Secretary of State, and notify the Michigan State Police and the applicant. At this point your conviction would be removed from your record, and you will receive a well-deserved fresh start.

Made in the USA
Monee, IL
04 November 2026

67386695R00085